Love of an Angel

Everything for a Reason Series Book 2

I0200545

By: Julie Edgington

Dedicated to Virginia C. Beard or,
as I knew her, Mom

Table of Contents

Author's Note vii

Chapter 1 | Tales of My First Adventures on Earth 1

Chapter 2 | Mom 7

Chapter 3 | Observing 17

Chapter 4 | Mother Memories 25

Chapter 5 | Innocence Lost 33

Chapter 6 | Letting Go 41

Chapter 7 | I Was Never Really Alone 49

Chapter 8 | Angels Among Us 57

Chapter 9 | A Guide to Creating Your Guides 65

Chapter 10 | Communicating with Your Guides and Angels 73

Epilogue 83

Author's Note

If you are new to the *Everything for a Reason* series, let me be the first to warmly welcome you. If you are continuing on along with me after our journey through Book 1, *Preacher's Li'l Secret,* I welcome you back again. In this series I share experiences of my life, not for the purpose of gaining an audience of people to commiserate with me, but to illustrate the truth many of us are coming to recognize: when you live your life according to the premise that everything that happens is for a reason and that we are spiritual beings on a path through the physical world, things fall into place and our lives begin to make sense to us.

As I shared in the first book of this series, I was abandoned my father. Mine is not an uncommon occurrence, sadly. As I worked out my own path of healing and coming to terms with what happened *to me*, doors of understanding and hope were opened and I finally realized that nothing happened *to me* and everything that's ever happened or ever will happen only occurs *because of me*. This includes the good, the bad and the ugly.

Taking control of our lives, relationships, thoughts, feelings and the situations we encounter and stepping into a deep understanding that we are the creators of our own life, are hallmark themes of my series. Whether you are new to the series or coming back again for the second book, I am grateful to share my journey with you. I hope once again my journey inspires you, motivates you, and changes you.

In this book in the series, I share my experience of dealing with a different kind of abandonment. Again, one that is not abnormal for many others, quite sadly. That is, the passing of my mother when I was quite young. This is a different kind of abandonment than that which comes when a parent knowingly and of their own volition vacates our life. The emotions are quite different because we not only are dealing with the loss of a parent and caregiver in our life, we are left also wondering all sorts of questions, like ***why me? Why now?***

Do the principles of healing from abandonment from a walk-away parent apply to those feelings of abandonment that come from a parent who passes away? My journey recorded here will touch on that question and take you into the depths of my own experience with this type of loss.

I believe I have found answers to questions that haunt many people. I look forward to sharing them with you here, in hopes they will help you to live your very best life.

Chapter 1

Tales of My First Adventures on Earth

"Children and mothers never truly part | Bound in the beating of each other's heart." [Charlotte Gray]

Even before my birth, God began testing me. He needed to know if I had the determination to be who this world needed me to be, someday. Would I have the courage to not only be the person who lived, but to tell my story? Within my story, there is proof that there is reason behind our life, our love and even our misfortune. I know without a doubt that we all, each of us, have a story to tell. More than the value of the story on its own, our stories are of supreme value when we pay attention to the most important part: ***Why are we telling our story?*** For me, my purpose in telling my story and in being tested the way I have been is for giving a different perspective on life, a perspective you might not receive anywhere else, from anyone. I am grateful for the courage to tell it.

I came into this world the usual way. I was a chubby, dark haired baby girl. The moment of my birth was the only moment in my life in which I was normal, untarnished and free of my limited beliefs. I wish I could go back to that moment. Sometimes I close my eyes and imagine what it was like to be that baby. As that baby, I imagine my only concern was to find my mother and nestle into her loving arms.

Little did I know as this innocent baby that life would be full of sorrow, twists, turns and constant tests of inner strength. I would spend most of my life in preparation for a catastrophic, yet wonderful, event. Only a life of tragedy and knowledge of unconditional love could help me withstand the explosive impact of events waiting ahead for me on my life's path. As a baby, I had no way to know that it would be many, many years before I would see that everything truly does happen for a reason, even seemingly horrible things.

My chance at life was given to me by my mother's courage and bravery. When Mom became pregnant with me, the doctor told her she should terminate the pregnancy or we would both die. Mom refused to have an abortion, no matter what reasons the doctor could give her for an abortion being a necessity. Mom never told me what led the doctor to his devastating and troubling diagnosis; I was never curious enough about it to ask. I remember thinking, *I'm here, and we're both alive; that's all that matters*.

Mom could have taken the easy way out. The doctor gave her every excuse and justification to end her pregnancy. I know it could not have been an easy decision for my mom, especially since the doctor's advice came only a short time after she had left my father to escape his abuse. She was on her own and already had two children at home and no family support system to help her. Adding a baby to the mix must have been terrifying.

Destiny played a role in how I came to be here, of that I am certain. Everything was orchestrated just right to bring about this little baby (me) to have the many experiences that were to come. Destiny is the name we give the contract we have made before we even come to this world. Within destiny, there are a great number of variables, but what never changes are the lessons we are served with through destiny's path. The lessons are the "written in stone" part of the contract and we cannot get past them.

No matter how hard we try to go down a different path in our life that is separate from what destiny has designed for us, in order to escape the sometimes painful lessons destiny is required to teach us, we will always end up at the same lessons. You can learn your lessons the hard way or the easy way, the choice is yours. Most of us, including me, choose the hard way. Why do we do that? I've often wondered.

Destiny put me into my mother's arms as a small baby. Destiny gave me a mother who was strong and every bit the person I needed her to be. To be best-equipped to handle the lessons destiny would present me with, I needed a mother who didn't scare easily, who selflessly put others before her own needs.

My mom was five feet, four inches tall and every inch of her was made up of pure stubbornness. It was Mom's stubbornness that allowed me to be here sharing this story with you. Mom had an unwavering faith in God that could not be budged. Even when her faith was challenged by the years of education her doctor possessed, she still held strong and chose a path her faith led her to.

As a child, I would get lost in the perfection of Mom's features as she told me the story of how I came to be here. Mom would proudly tell me the story of her confrontation with the doctor with her head held high. "They told me that I should have an abortion, but I knew you would be just fine. The doctors told me that both of us, you and I, would die if I brought you into this world." Mom would continue the story with just a hint of wretchedness in her voice, clearly still holding some contempt for the doctor even years later. The tone she used in regards to the story of my birth was the same one she used when she knew someone was wrong; her square-shaped nose would crinkle ever so slightly. "The doctor told me if by chance we both lived, you would have a lot of problems and wouldn't have much of a life."

The tone in her voice would go from sadness to something bordering on pompousness. Squinting her almond-shaped eyes just slightly she would say, "I knew that the doctors were wrong and even if they were not, well that was the way God wanted it."

Mom was an intelligent person who could not be intimidated by much. She never let me have the slightest clue she was scared when making the decision she made to keep me. She would perk up as she told the next part of my story. "When you were born the doctor laid you on a cold metal table, with not so much as even a blanket!" The doctor and nurses were tending to Mom first, which she did not like at all. She yelled, "Get my baby off that metal table and take care of her, not me!"

Could being stuck on that cold metal table have been my first taste of abandonment? It sure wouldn't be my last. Thinking about the feeling of loneliness, a feeling I sometimes enjoy and sometimes fear, makes me think of that baby, laying there cold and shocked by her first glimpse of her brand new world.

Mom also told me how dumbfounded the hospital staff was when they discovered I was healthy and normal. Well, I was *almost* normal. There was a little problem with my legs and feet. I was pigeon-toed and the doctor would later put casts on my legs to correct the problem. To look at me now, you would never guess that my feet were almost turned completely backwards when I was born.

Mom would always follow the story of my birth with the story of how one nurse gave her the wrong baby. Mom received a Hispanic baby girl in my place. "I knew that other baby was not you. I would have known you anywhere!" Mom would start laughing in a playful way as she shared this part of our first adventure together. "You could be Hispanic right now, living a totally different life."

In hindsight, replaying Mom's story of my birth, I sometimes wonder if the "baby switch" incident wasn't coincidental at all. As in, maybe it was God giving me one more chance to get out of the life which was set before me. Maybe He wanted to give me a chance to change my contract, my destiny, because He knew it was going to be very difficult. Maybe God wanted to make sure I was serious about my mission. I've come now to realize my mission is an important one, though not an easy one, and includes taking care of one of God's most precious beings. It also includes realizing when it was time to grow and have a rebirth of thoughts, feelings and emotions. And I, being the somewhat supercilious person that I am, accepted the lifelong experience of being me and am grateful my mom spoke up and prevented the baby swap that would have changed all that.

When I was young, I did not care about the fact that I was never supposed to be born, according to the doctor. I did not care that I almost went home with the wrong family. All I cared about was hearing Mom tell my story. It was a story that was unique, cherished and beloved because, in the self-centric way of children, it had me as the subject. I didn't know it then, but each time Mom told me that story, she was creating and reinstalling an important belief.

Through her story, my mom taught me this: if you deeply and truly believe in something, no matter what it is, it will turn out the way you know it will, the way you want it to. Sometimes, if you are open and don't worry about what can happen, it can turn out even better than you expected. What has to happen first is, we have to refuse to take someone else's word and refuse to accept things as we are told they are supposed to be. What happens next is standing strong in your knowledge that *you* are the one who will determine what will happen. My mom did this without even knowing she was doing it! Mom gave me the belief of faith. Having trust in faith would give me the first tool I needed to survive life. After all, faith is the stepping stone between surviving and thriving.

Whether it was teaching me an unknown lesson or making me feel special by telling me the story of being the baby of the family, I loved any and all attention my mom gave me. She loved giving attention to me, as much as I loved receiving it. All I had to do was smile at her and her face would light up. I knew when I grew up I wanted to be just like her, so loving and caring and always putting everyone else first. Even wanting to be just like Mom would become a lesson all unto itself throughout my life. Trying to live up to a person so great leaves its toll on your soul, which of course makes up a part of who I am.

Chapter 2

Mom

"The Universe is one great kindergarten for man. Everything that exists has brought with it its own peculiar lesson."
[Orison Swett Marden]

There is nothing I wouldn't give to hear Mom tell my story again. I miss the comforting sound of her voice almost as much as her smile. Her smile was one-of-a-kind; it would light up a city block if you could harness its energy. To go along with her stellar smile, Mom was a classic beauty and had the charm of a queen. Her fierce determination, combined with her other wonderful attributes, meant she could and did anything she set her mind to.

As comfortable fishing and fixing things as she was at throwing fancy parties, Mom was a beautiful mix of capability, extravagance and generosity, all rolled up into the soul of a dreamer. And yet, she was down to earth and approachable, and sometimes harsh at the same time. She had a sense of humor that has been irreplaceable in my life. She had horrible judgment when it came to picking a man. She always seemed to love the wrong ones. She could be bossy at times, but now I recognize that her bossiness was simply her way of insisting that she stood up and spoke her mind, no matter what the consequences. And some may call this a flaw, her outspoken nature, but the sum total of who Mom was overshadows any perceived flaws. Compared to anyone else I have ever met, Mom was angelic.

Mom is actually the reason I believe in angels. I am not talking about archangels that are magical and mystical (though they certainly do have a special place in this world); I am talking about the real life angels that walk this earth. You probably know someone like this too. If so, you probably also agree that angels aren't perfect and, just like the rest of us, they wonder why they are here. But if you have met one, you will know exactly what they are. They take on the tough experiences in life which need to be experienced for the whole. I believe we are all one and nothing in our shared experience is separate unto us. Angels sacrifice themselves to experience things to help aid the rest of us, so we don't have to make the tough decisions, like dying and leaving behind our children so they can learn their lessons.

It isn't just the adverse, challenging things angels tackle that make them angels. It also has to do with how they seem to come through every situation with a greater sense of knowing, which is shared with all of the rest of us. Angels know how to survive horrible situations, happy situations, beautiful situations, and survive them by seeing everything in a new and different way. Because of their rich experiences, angels somehow seem to have all the answers, no matter what, even when bad things take their toll on the spirit of an angel. Through it all, angels rebound in a short time and snap out of any and every situation quickly and not beaten down, but stronger. Is it possible you are an angel? Is it possible you know one in your life?

Mom never had an easy life and it showed. It showed not in the way she looked, but in how she acted. For example, she was a firm believer in tough love, especially with her kids. She wanted us to grow up to be good people, like most parents do, but the strength of soul that raising kids requires came from years of her own heartbreak. Mom grew up with a stepmother who didn't like her very much and a father who never cared. One time, I asked Mom about her family and her childhood, as I was curious to know why we didn't ever spend time with any of her relatives. I have never met any of my aunts, uncles, cousins or grandparents, from either side of my parents' families. Mom explained why.

"When I was young," she said, "my stepmother got in my face and told me how much she hated me." I felt bad for my mom after that and sad that she did not have a mother to love her, like she loved me.

8

I don't know what happened to my mom's birth mother, but I am sure it left my mother with abandonment issues of her own. Related to her father, Mom had another set of problems, which I don't know all the details of, but which I recently received some clues about. Just as I started to write this chapter, I was given an envelope full of pictures which had belonged to my mom. I had never before seen these pictures and as I looked at them I realized it was the first time I had ever seen what my mom's family looked like. Some were of her dad. In just about every picture which contained her father's face, scribble marks were there, as if by obscuring his face from the photos she could erase him from her life. As I said, I'm not sure exactly what happened between them but, unfortunately, whatever it was, they were never able to rectify it.

My mom got married when she was just 16 years old. She married a man who ultimately became abusive and who ended up taking her first child from her, my sister Deb. I recently learned that her first husband also forced her to give up a baby boy for adoption. I know it must have torn her up to do so as Mom loved her children more than anything in this world. I imagine this is where Mom gained some of her stronger characteristics, such as never allowing anyone to tell her what to do ever again, and speaking her mind no matter what the consequences.

After she became divorced from her first husband, she remarried a couple more times, each man just as wonderful to her as the last (I hope you can sense my sarcasm). She even endured one husband killing himself. Starting with her own father, the men in my mom's life never treated her well.

By the time I came along, Mom was in her thirties. You would think she would have closed herself away from the world after all she had endured in her short years up to that point, but she didn't. She kept her sense of humor and her generosity. Unfortunately, she also kept her limiting belief regarding how she thought she should be treated by men. I am sure those limiting beliefs were created by a childhood spent watching her own father mistreat her mother, her stepmother, and probably her as well. Sadly, she never was able to break through and overcome those limiting beliefs that led her to think she didn't

9

deserve to be treated well by a man, and that altruistic, true, kind love was possible for her.

At the time I was born, my mom was living in California. She had had moved there after leaving my father and was working third shift at a bakery. My brother Kenny, who was ten at the time, would watch my second oldest sister, Cindy, who was seven years old, and me, just a newborn baby, while Mom was at work. I would keep Kenny up all night and Mom up all day because I had colic and cried constantly. Mom was on the verge of a nervous breakdown.

In that same envelope of pictures I was recently given, there was a letter from my mom to my sister Deb, who was sixteen at the time and living with her grandparents. In the letter, my mother was trying to tell my sister about my birth. She explained how hard and scary it was that she almost died when I was born. Mom wrote how desperate and lost she felt being all alone to take care of a new baby and two other kids all by herself. My mother didn't tell Deb any of this to gain her sympathy. Rather, she was explaining her circumstances to Deb in order to prove a point. My mom said to my sister in the note, "In all things, thank God."

She went on to explain to my sister we must thank God for everything we go through, even the bad experiences. Why, you might wonder, should we thank God for the bad experiences? Well, He has allowed those experiences to come to us because we are here to experience them. We get the privilege of learning and growing from the experiences he gives us. These experiences, good and bad, are bringing up what you are trying to manifest. If you are continually not grateful in all things, then there will not be a break in your vibrational match between what you're experiencing and what you desire. Through your less than desirable circumstances, you have the opportunity to envision how you want your life to be and raise your vibration to attract a new and different outcome.

Of course, the lessons we must learn through these experiences aren't always pretty or nice. I'm not saying we should disregard those miserable feelings, and sometimes we need to spend some time feeling and acknowledging our sadness and misery. Sometimes, you just need to sit right down and feel sorry for yourself. After all, if we don't *feel* those things that come as a result of our experiences, if we don't allow ourselves to deeply sense all that comes as a result of our current, miserable circumstances, we cheat ourselves out of the total experience we need to learn from at that moment. But, if we stay too long in that negative vibration, we risk getting stuck there. What I've learned is, we need to go with the flow, even if it is negative, and then remember to find a way out of our tears and sorrow before we get stuck too long in them. And always continue to be grateful, even if it is just being grateful for the chance to experience what you don't want, so that you will be brought into knowing what you *do* want. Keep the faith, no matter what, and you will get to your manifestation!

It took Mom the desperation of wanting to give up on life, but not being able to because of her beliefs about how much she loved her children, to figure out how to be grateful in all things and why this was such an important lesson. Once she figured it out, she reached a place in her experience where she could survive just about anything.

Mom kept her faith and when I was about six months old, we moved to Iowa. In Iowa, back in a place Mom considered home, Mom must have been excited to have some help and support from friends and find some relief from bearing our family burden alone. I remember when I was growing up Mom would always say, "You can try to leave Waterloo, but you will always come back to it." Waterloo, Iowa, is the literal Waterloo she spoke of, but I think it can also be taken figuratively. For Mom, Waterloo was her safety net. No matter how hard she tried to leave, which was a lot, she would always come back here. Mom couldn't seem to ever settle down. Even when she was at home in Waterloo, she had this itch to keep moving. It seemed just as we would finally get settled, my mom would find something she thought was just a little bit better. She always wanted better for us and never stopped trying for it.

For myself, having seen my mom's relentless search for a home that was better, I know now that "home" is not a place in this world, rather it's a feeling you get when you are loved and belong. In a way, to justify how much we moved, Mom would tell me at a very early age, "As long as we are together, anywhere is home."

After living in Iowa for a few years, Mom began dating La Vern. La Vern was an old flame and very familiar to my mom. After having to take care of us all by herself, I think she just became so exhausted and Vern was a distraction from her misery. Vern, as I used to call him, was an answer to her prayers. It wasn't that Vern was ideal, but I am sure being with him and having his help beat being alone.

Vern was a man my mom had married long before I was born. She had married and divorced him before she met my father. Mom just could not seem to resist whatever it was she saw in him. I'm sure it was her need to be treated like her father treated her. Or, maybe she craved the attention her father never gave her and saw her chance to try and earn something from Vern that, sadly, he would never be able to give her either. It is an urge I know all too well. There is an attraction to something you know is wrong deep down inside, but you can't resist the attraction.

I've come to learn this attraction comes from limiting beliefs created when you are young, beliefs that come from watching the most important woman in your life get treated horribly by men. It wires your brain in such a way that you think that is the way it is *supposed to be*, and so you desire what you see as normal, even when you know it is destructive and wrong. This is something that gets passed down from generation to generation, from one woman to the next. We want so much to be like our mothers and gain the attention of our fathers, so some of us grow up craving to be treated like we are worthless, always striving for the approval of careless men, hoping against hope that the attention we seek isn't so unobtainable after all. There are men out there that will treat women as equals, some will even treat women like a queen, but they will not seem as desirable because everyone wants someone or something they just can't have. Vern definitely treated Mom like she wasn't wanted. Although, by the look of him, Vern should have treated my mother like she was a rare treasure.

Vern was a short, old man with a great American comb over, as my older sister Cindy and I used to call it. A "great American comb over" is when the hair on one side of a man's head is at least six inches long and he uses it to patch over the top of his balding head. That one flap of hair would sometimes get caught by the wind and we knew it was just a matter of time before the crust from his hair gel weakened. Once the gel was weak enough, the whole thing would get blown back over to its rightful side.

Vern was diabetic, which caused him to have problems with his feet and legs. He walked hunched over and leaning on his cane. A chain smoker, Vern would already be lighting up the next cigarette before he even finished the one he'd started. And yet, having health problems, serious ones, didn't stop him from being mean to Mom. He worked hard to make her life miserable, and he succeeded. He tried to be physically abusive, as much as a crippled old man can be, but mentally he beat her up every single day. Vern went above and beyond treating Mom badly. He was, quite simply, crazy.

Of all the horrid things I saw occur in my mom's relationship with Vern, one story sticks out in my mind the most. Mom and Vern owned some real estate, mostly consisting of rental properties. When I was three, shortly after they had remarried, we were living in one of the rental properties. I have heard this story a hundred times from Cindy and to this day, it still gives me the creeps just thinking about it.

The kids, including me, and Mom were in one of the bedrooms taking a nap when Mom was awakened by the sound of me coughing. She smelled something and after some investigation, she realized the smell was from the pilot lights being out and the gas was still turned on. The house was filling with gas and Mom quickly got her kids out. Once we were outside the house, the cause of the gas leak was found. It was Vern.

No, he did not have digestive problems. He had blown out all the pilot lights on the stove and turned the gas all the way up! Of course, he denied having anything to do with the pilots being out and the gas being turned on, but when he was found, he was sitting in the attic smoking cigars. I don't know if Mom really believed him when he said he hadn't done it, or if it was because it was her belief that if you kept quiet and pretended your family was normal no one would notice it wasn't. It might sound silly that anyone could actually believe people wouldn't notice how **not normal** your family was, but it was the early 80s then and people actually thought that way. There was a pervasive opinion that you didn't air your dirty laundry. Or, maybe Mom just hoped no one could truly be that crazy or mean that they would try to kill their entire family.

I do know that Mom always tried to see the good in people, even if there just wasn't any there. This is probably where I picked up my beliefs about always needing to find good in every person, which sometimes can be a limiting belief, but it has allowed me to see the good in every situation and take a lesson from any event, even the ones that are difficult.

It has taken some time, but I can finally say that events in my adult life have given me some perspective on my mom's relationship with Vern. For some time, I wondered what limited beliefs cause men, or anyone for that matter, to be so careless with someone else's feelings, like Vern was with my mom's. Being curious, asking questions and wondering about things, allows the universe to bring answers through experiences. Many years later, I met a man who gave me the experience of being challenged to see past the way he treated me. I had to learn to see past his actions and his ill treatment of me because of a love so strong it takes on a mind of its own. Learning to step back and put away judgment allowed me to see why he treated me the way he did, and gave me some perspective on Mom's and Vern's relationship.

Part of the lesson involved not taking everything so personally. Thinking about the past and what conditions people to behave a certain way gave me a sense of understanding. What this man taught me was how to forgive and what forgiveness means. Stubbornness and pain had gotten in the way, and that was a lesson too. You are only hurting yourself if you don't keep an open mind and open heart. And part of being open is allowing things to happen, including love.

The man in my life had been hurt by his own mother at a very young age, through things she had done and through eventually abandoning

14

him as if he wasn't good enough to keep in her life. However, when he was still just a child, he learned to love his stepmother, or his "real mother" as he calls her. I believe she was another angel, just like my own mother, put here on earth to help teach a lesson. His stepmother died of cancer when she was very young. He was abandoned again, except this time his hurt and pain didn't start his belief of not being good enough to keep a loving woman in his life, it confirmed it and made it stronger. His belief is this: if he loves a woman too much, she will just leave, causing unbearable heartache. So, he never allows a woman too close. Just before he feels tempted to love a woman and allow her to be close to him, he does hurtful things to make sure she will not want to be loved by him. He needed to learn he was good enough just as he is to make a woman want to stay. He thought he was looking for unconditional love. He wanted unconditional love because he was in conflict with himself; he wanted to love and be loved, but his beliefs wouldn't allow it. To him, unconditional love meant he could do any hurtful thing he wanted and a woman would stay. It also meant he thought he could have what he wanted without changing his belief. And I completely understand how awful it can feel to change a belief, even one that is hurting us. In his case, change was scary because it meant he was risking abandonment and pain. It was scary for him that being in the misery of not allowing himself to be loved was more comfortable. I think most of us recognize these feelings associated with change.

Many years later, when I came into this man's life, he had no intention of falling in love. He truly had given up on having a relationship, but what we didn't know at the time was that we needed each other to learn our lessons. He was ideal for me because he was the man who fit my beliefs. He was, in a sense, my father in that I had to earn his love and no matter what I did to please him, it wasn't going to be enough for him ever love me. Loving him allowed me to see that my subconscious mind was playing out the events of my relationship just exactly as I thought it should be. We fit perfectly together, like puzzle pieces, or like a script written for a movie that was a whirlwind of our respective beliefs. I would try and try to gain his love, he would never love me the way I wanted because if he loved me too much, then I would somehow go away. The more he didn't love me, the more desperately I worked to earn his love. And round and round we went in this vicious cycle.

Looking objectively at our situation, you might think we just should not have been together. He would do things to hurt me and I would just keep allowing myself to get hurt. Really what was going on, what you would not be able to have seen from the outside, was that we were both simply unwilling to question our beliefs and our reality. It is that resistance to learning our lessons that keeps us stuck in them.

Our lessons in this relationship were plentiful. I needed to learn that I am lovable and worth it, just as I am. He needed to learn women don't leave because he loves them and that he is worth sticking around for. Without knowing it, we have taught each other so many lessons. Who knows what will happen to us, but whatever happens I am grateful to have learned so much about myself through this relationship. Situations like this are why we are here. This is what we call life. It is not just happening randomly, everything in life is for a reason. Those reasons and discovering those reasons are the experience of life.

As I said earlier, I have been able to understand my mom and Vern a little better through my own relationship. The insight I've gained is that just like any other relationship, it wasn't all bad for Mom and Vern. I also understand a bit more about the vicious cycle they must have been stuck in. At the least, Vern was the closest thing I ever had to knowing what it is like to have a dad and even though he was a very poor example of a dad, he sure has given me some interesting stories to tell.

Chapter 3

Observing

"Early in life I learned, just through observation, that right always wins out over wrong. If a person has good intentions in his heart and wants to do the right thing, then there are certain ways that any obstacle can be overcome."
[Monte Irvin]

When I was three Mom and Vern moved us from Iowa to Arkansas. I am sure it was Mom's idea. She must have thought if we had a change of scenery things between her and Vern would get better. In Arkansas we lived in a space with a huge acreage, surrounded by open space and lots of farm animals. Being that I was so little, about all I can remember is being excited to be going someplace new. I was never scared and didn't miss anyone back in Iowa because just about everyone I knew had gone with us, except my sister Debbie and her husband Curt, but I didn't know them that well.

In Arkansas I fell in love with the animals. It wasn't long before all the animals became my best friends. The animals were my escape from any bad feelings I ever had. And if I had something happy to share, they were there for that too. I had my own pony, I don't remember calling him anything, but "my pony". I loved seeing the baby chicks hatch. My number one best friend was a wild turkey my mom fittingly called Tom. Vern just showed up with him one day a few weeks before Thanksgiving. It wasn't just that I loved Tom, he loved me too. I was the only one he would allow in his cage. Every morning I would go outside, get in his cage and sit there with him in the crisp November air. I would sing silent night, the only song

I knew at that age, and it would never fail that Tom would gobble right along. I would spend hours in Tom's cage with him. Mom would send my brother out to get me for lunch. Every time, Tom would try to attack him when he would come up to the cage. Mom eventually learned to just give me my lunch in Tom's cage. Mom would bring my lunch to me and Tom didn't care who she was or what she was doing, he would go after her too.

Anyone who tried to get me out of that cage was met with Tom's big puffed out chest and a loud thundering thump, coming somewhere from inside him. It seemed to be connected to the earth somehow. You could feel that sound inside your body and it would make your hair stand on end. That same sound everyone else was terrified of, I found to be comforting. I knew being in that cage with Tom meant there was nothing in the world that could hurt me and no one could make me do anything I didn't want to do. I was protected and safe. But my time with my turkey friend was too short. Thanksgiving came and went. Tom wasn't in his cage anymore. I have never felt protected like that ever again. My last day with Tom was the last day I ever felt safe in life. I know it seems ridiculous because he was just a turkey, right? My opinion is this: angels don't just come in human form; they are all around us, protecting us, giving us what we need when we need it and when we ask for it.

Mom was happy when we first moved. She loved doing things like making homemade root beer – the best I've ever had – and growing and canning her own foods. We were having the time of our life in Arkansas and that place and time hold some of my fondest childhood memories. And they even sometimes include Vern. Not all my stories about my stepdad are horrific; in fact, there are some that to do this day still make me laugh. It is as if there is some divine humor in our circumstances and that somehow the Universe knew I would need to have a solid foundation of laughable memories in life to get me through.

My brother Kenny was usually behind most of that humor. He definitely knew if he could do something, anything, to get revenge on Vern and make Mom smile, it was a win-win situation. I often use the following scenario in my mind whenever I am feeling down, to cheer myself up. Vern, being the arrogant jerk that he was, was trying to lasso a calf from the back of an old pick-up truck while Kenny was driving. Vern thought he knew how to lasso a calf, but it was only because he thought he knew how to do everything. To my knowledge I am pretty sure this was Vern's first attempt at playing cowboy. I was in the back of the pick-up truck with Vern. I must have been about four at the time. Kenny was driving us across our big, open and hilly farm where there were cows grazing.

I can remember one minute Vern was standing there in the back of the pick-up truck yelling something and swinging the rope in the air. The next minute, my brother hit a bump that was small, but it was a big enough bump to jostle Vern and he flew out of the back of the truck! We came to an abrupt stop as soon as my brother realized what had happened. And there was Vern, rolling down the long, steep hill towards a little creek that ran through the field. I'll never forget the sight of Vern's arms and legs flopping around as his body bounced down the hill. We could hear the sound of muffled, breathless cuss words coming from the rag doll that was now Vern as he rolled, rolled, rolled away.

Not surprisingly, our first reaction was **not** to race down the hill after Vern and offer our assistance or try to minimize the impact of his rolling. Rather, Kenny was almost dying from laughter in the driver's seat of the old pick-up truck. And I, well, I just sat there, stunned, with my eyes wide open, waiting to see if he was ever going to stop rolling. Vern did finally stop rolling once he hit the creek and he was alright. Kenny was not going to be though, not by the look on Vern's face. Vern was furious.

Thanks to my mom's quick thinking, Kenny did not get in trouble at all. Instead, she made Vern feel like a fool for having tried the stupid stunt – lassoing in the back of a moving truck, on a back road – and made my brother out to be the innocent victim of that bump that got in his way. I knew Kenny had probably done it on purpose, just to get back at Vern, but as Mom put it, "What kind of idiot would stand in the back of a truck while a 14-year old kid was driving?" That incident is one of the funniest things I have ever witnessed. And, I'm not too proud to say, I am guilty of getting a little pleasure from another's misfortune. I am only human, and Vern was a menace and an all-around jerk, so he probably had it coming.

When I was five, we moved back to Iowa. I was sad to leave Arkansas and all the animals I had come to know as my friends. However it did feel like we were going home. Maybe I had picked up on that feeling coming from my mom or maybe I had at this point already picked up my mother's bad habit of not being able to stay in one place too long. As such a young child I got very used to not having a say in what happened in my life or to me. Even at that young of an age, I just went with the flow and learned to swallow the sorrow of losing something I had found so happy and comforting.

The abuse towards Mom and the fighting with Vern became much worse once back in Iowa. I remember looking at Vern one time when he was in a rage towards Mom. They had been arguing about money which wasn't uncommon. Vern had his fair share of money and was very obsessive over it. I had stopped what I was doing and had a "deer in the headlights" gaze when I looked in his eyes. I was only a little girl at the time, but vivid are the feelings you can't forget when you see a man's eyes change colors from brown to red. It was during that same fight that I watched Vern throw handfuls of money into the fireplace. Vern defiantly loved being dramatic and Mom loved showing him how in control she was by not over reacting to his theatrical actions. Of course, her lack of emotions would cause Vern to become even angrier. As a child collecting beliefs I am sure I learned money equals problems. The more you have, the more problems you will have. Or, another belief for me is, money turns men into monsters. I could go on, but you get the idea. What statements feel true to you about money?

What kind of limited beliefs are created in a small child observing the abuse of their own mother and watching her stand up for herself constantly? Is this where I learned to speak up for myself? Is this why my mouth seems to run on its own whenever I see an injustice in the world? Probably so.

Asking all these questions of myself and always wondering are part of what has led me to want to tell my story. I know there are others

20

out there who are lost and curious as to why they do the things they do, too. Having written my thoughts down most of my life has made it easier for me to go back and see patterns and realize that there is reason for our current actions, with the reasons rooted in the past, and there is a why. This has strengthened the observer in me.

Back in Iowa again, Cindy and Kenny were getting older and it wasn't long before they starting stepping in and sticking up for Mom. Vern would never have laid a hand on any of us kids, and we all knew it. His style towards us kids was more passive-aggressive anyway, like trying to start a gas fire in the house with us in it. And even if he had tried to harm us, Cindy and Kenny were old enough and big enough that they could have stopped him. They simply were not going to allow Vern to hurt Mom anymore. The tension was definitely building in our little family and I think Mom knew that if she did not get rid of Vern, he would end up hurting our family somehow, someway, or even worse, killing someone.

I was just a little over six years old when Mom divorced Vern, for the second time. I was so happy that he was not living with us anymore. So many beliefs were created in me before I was even old enough to know what a belief is. For example, I learned that it's okay to be treated like garbage, as long as it is a sacrifice you are making for your children so they can be taken care of. And, I learned that life is full of drama and misery and that it is noble and desirable to put yourself in situations where you can emerge a survivor.

None of those beliefs I accumulated from observing Mom and Vern are healthy, I know it. And, it has taken me years to unravel them and overcome them. I don't think we ever completely overcome them. But I succumbed to them as truths for a good long time in my own adult life before having the wisdom and strength to even attempt to transform them.

After Vern left our life, Mom was working all the time doing one of the things she did best, being a chef. She had to support us by herself again, but now that I was older I think it was easier for her to be away at work more. I would not understand until years later how difficult it must have been for Mom to make that choice, to kick Vern out of our lives. The financial strain it put on her was not insignificant, and I'm sure she must have known what challenges lay ahead of her by divorcing Vern. And beyond financially being solely responsible for us, she must have been so lonely, even with her kids around. I am sure the loneliness is what Mom probably feared the most. She was strong and she knew what she had to do, and she would always do what she needed to no matter how hard it was, but it must have been lonely for her without a partner, even an abusive one.

Still, I think she began to learn she was more comfortable and things were less complicated when she didn't have a man around. I came to see Mom as an independent person who took care of everything all by herself. Mom never really had to count on anyone, not unless she absolutely needed to. This new life became my new normal, seeing my Mom do it all by herself. Of course, this too created beliefs in me. I observed and learned and became comfortable with the idea of a woman surviving on her own and being independent.

After Vern left, Mom had boyfriends here and there, sporadically. Nothing was serious though, until she met Francis. Mom dated Francis for some time before I actually met him, when I was about 8 years old. Francis was an older, funny looking man and the best way I can describe him would be to ask you to conjure up an image of Bozo the Clown. He had Bozo's hair and nose at least, certainly. Mom had a knack for picking men who were not exactly the GQ kind, despite the fact that she definitely deserved GQ.

Francis was a cheap man, the kind of man that wouldn't spend an extra dime on his lady if he didn't have to. He would take Mom to church for free dinners on date nights, for example. Needless to say, I did not like Francis. And though he never verbalized it, I knew he didn't like me much either. I knew this because he would do things like change the TV back to football so I would leave the room. Back in those days, there was only one TV in the entire house. As I would walk up the stairs, I would hear him turn the TV back to the show I had been watching. If I came back downstairs, it would get changed to football again. I knew he did little things like this to make my life miserable. He made me feel as if I was just something in the way.

I figured Francis out quickly. He knew I wouldn't say anything to Mom about how he had me feel and the little jabs he constantly poked at me with, like TV and football to get me to leave the room. In return, I also know he couldn't say anything to Mom about my shenanigans either. Like the time I offered him a plastic apple. When he tried to bite into it, he almost broke a tooth. Or the time I gave him a trick taffy that was made mostly of salt. The bad part about the taffy was, he ate it and he liked it! He probably only ate it because it was free. I still got a laugh out of the fact that he was so cheap that he would eat nasty stuff, like trick taffy, just because it was free.

Thankfully Mom never did have him move in with us. He had his house and she had hers. That was definitely the way Francis like it. He wasn't a stellar boyfriend to be sure, but he didn't hit mom or mentally abuse her, and that was probably all that mattered to Mom, sadly. It truly is sad when a woman gives up trying to find her true love and settles for someone practical, with their only saving grace being that they don't hit her. Oh yes, I was observing, taking it all in. Those beliefs were accumulating, creating mountains of beliefs I would carry into my own adult life, just from watching Mom.

Despite her poor choices regarding men and the types of beliefs this created in me and surely in my siblings as well, I know that Mom was always trying for a better life, even if it meant she had to be with someone who wasn't exactly Prince Charming, or putting up with someone being crazy. Even when it meant she had to work all the time and be lonely so that we would have everything we needed, no matter what Mom always gave us unconditional love and lots of laughter because we were hers. It did not matter how many mistakes Mom made, she was and always will be my angel.

Chapter 4

Mother Memories

*"The mother memories that are closest to my heart are the small
gentle ones that I have carried over from the days of my childhood.
They are not profound, but they have stayed with me through life,
and when I am very old, they will still be near."*
[Margaret Sanger]

Mom was only here on this earth for a short time. In the time we
had together though, she taught me so much – how to be funny,
how to be strong, and the importance of keeping an open mind. She
taught me that it is okay to make mistakes, and how to deal with
them when you do. The things she taught me are innumerable, but
the most important of all is that she taught me how to love and how
to never give up.

It's never easy for a child, or anyone, to understand why we have
to say goodbye to those we love. And yet, many years later, I am
now able to see the reasoning behind Mom leaving me behind at
such a young age. God's intention was not to put me through the
pain of losing my mom for the sake of pain alone; rather, allowing
me to go through losing my mom laid a foundation for my future. I
was going to need a great deal of will power and a strong belief in
God to handle many things my future held, and this is how God and
Mom gave me both.

It was Thanksgiving 1985. I was nine years old and looking
forward to Mom's famous Thanksgiving feast. As the head chef of
a local, high end restaurant, Mom's cooking was five-stars. Like
Thanksgiving Day feasts in the past, we would have it all – from

turkey to pumpkin pie and everything in between. The smell of onions, gravy and sweetness coming from Mom's kitchen always sent my nasal passages on a wonderful, anticipatory ride.

At that time, Kenny was grown and had moved out; Cindy, being able to drive, was gone most of the time like a typical teenager. When Francis wasn't around, it was just Mom and me, but around the holidays everyone was home, even Deb and her husband Curt, because nobody wanted to miss Mom's cooking. This year the holiday was a little different though. There was a tension in the air that I couldn't explain and didn't understand as a child. Everyone seemed upset and argumentative, but no one would tell me what was wrong. I must have decided to try and not let it bother me though, rationalizing that whatever was wrong would go away eventually, like things had a way of doing in our lives. What I know now is, everyone was trying to protect me from something that was about to become a huge part of my life and shape who I would eventually become.

The monster everyone was protecting me from was cancer. Mom had lung cancer. Mom had come down with pneumonia and through the course of being treated for it, cancer had also been discovered. I don't even recall Mom being sick at all, not with pneumonia, not with anything. That's how strong she was. Just as before, she never would let me know by words or deeds that anything was wrong. But that changed. Seeing her become sick was something none of us could avoid.

For two years, I watched as Mom became a person who had cancer. Her skin yellowed. She took dozens of pills every day – some were prescribed to her by a doctor, some were things like nutritional supplements such as garlic that she took with the hope that it would help her live longer. Despite the pills and no matter how hard she tried, I could tell that she was always tired. And yet, some things didn't change: she always tried to make the best of a bad situation.

I watched my mom lose a lot of weight. It was as if it was just melting away, taking her with it. Even this was used as an opportunity to be bright and cheery and I remember she talked about how she was so proud of finally losing weight and that she finally had won her battle with being overweight. It scared me though. Mom had always been thin, until after she gave birth to me. Then, she gained quite a bit of weight. I never knew Mom as skinny until she had cancer. As a child, I was overweight and this was something she and I shared. I watched my mother become skinny while I continued to gain weight, and it was scary. I began to feel more alone than ever.

Mom dealt with her illness the only way she knew how – with a twisted but funny sense of humor. This is probably where I learned how to make fun of bad things and just put it all out there in a blunt, funny way to ease my own pain. For example, when Mom started losing her hair from chemotherapy, she made a big joke about it. I remember one day when Cindy and I came home from school, we threw our backpacks down in the entry way. We walked up the stairs to the living room and Mom was sitting in her usual spot on the couch, waiting for us to come home. I knew as soon as I saw her, the look on her face, that she had something up her sleeve. I'd seen her play jokes on us before.

"You kids are driving me crazy! So crazy I could just pull my hair out!" Mom said, trying to hide her laughter. Then she grabbed a handful of brown, short, curly hair and actually pulled a big clump right out of her head! She held her hand up in the air, shaking it at us as if she was serious and furious. Mom and I broke out in laughter. Cindy, being older and more mature, didn't think it was funny at all. Now that I think about it, I still think it was funny. Is there a more humorous way to tell your kids that all of your hair is going to fall out because of your damn therapy that never even worked anyway?

In actuality, Mom was upset about losing her hair, as much as she tried to make light of it. She probably spent half a day crying about losing her hair. As a person who took great pride in how she looked, losing her beautiful hair must have broken her heart. The other half of the day she probably spent trying to figure out how she was going to tell us in a way that was lighthearted but meaningful, knowing her. Mom wanted us to learn a lesson through her experience that would stay with us our whole lives. That is, laughter and love is and always has been the very best medicine. Through her, we learned not to sit around crying about the bad stuff, and how to turn the bad stuff around and own it. When you own something, you can do whatever you want with it. She was always looking for an opportunity to teach us something about life, which is what happens when you believe everything happens for a reason.

Another message Mom made very clear is this: live each day to its fullest. No matter how bad she felt, she always found some way to make each day special. Some days were special because we would just sit together on a Thursday night watching Cosby, Cheers and Night Court, which we loved so much. Mom would take me to do special things too and it would be just the two of us. Picnics and horseback riding were both our favorites.

The special days Mom and I had together did not mask the sleepless nights of agony I know she had to endure. I would sleep with mom so we wouldn't feel so alone. I would get up in the middle of the night with mom and rub her back as she laid there holding back the tears from all the pain. She refused to ever let me see her cry, and I never did. She believed crying was a sign of weakness. Even though she seemed to struggle with every breath she took, she would just lay there. I would lay next to her at night listening to her breathe. The sound of the wheezing coming from her lungs made my stomach turn as I knew there was something wrong, but never knew what. It was as if someone had her in a constant bear hug and she could not break free. I would rub her back for her until she fell asleep. Sometimes I would continue to rub her back even after she fell asleep, just so she would still know I was there.

During those nights I learned of my own need to make someone feel better and I learned how to keep trying until they do. Some might find my constant need to take care of my loved ones and make them comfortable annoying, but when I see someone in pain I am whisked away to a time when I was 9 years old and watched as my mother suffered and I was the only one there who could help. As I stated in *Preacher's Li'l Secret*, when we have traumatic events when we are children we get stuck in that moment and we can't grow beyond it.

I remember going to the hospital after Mom had her left lung removed. Mom had even put on a happy face on for me then. I was curious and I asked mom if I could see her cut. The incision the doctor had made was from the top of her chest, down and around her side, all the way up her back. It looked like a puzzle piece that had been stapled into place. I saw all the staples and I was scared. When she came home I didn't want to hug her out of fear that I would hurt her. Fear of pain did not stop her from hugging me though.

Since I have become a mother, I wonder if the physical sickness Mom felt paled in comparison to the pain of knowing she would have to leave me behind to face the world without her. I was the baby and not old enough to be on my own yet. I fear leaving my children behind at all, ever, let alone before they are grown. I have had to learn how to not live in that fearful place of hoping it doesn't happen, and instead I try to enjoy the moments, good and bad.

Mom was one tough cookie, always hiding her pain no matter what kind of pain it was. I never had a clue she was scared. She never even gave me the idea that she thought she was going to die from the cancer. Every night before we went to sleep, Mom and I would pray to God. When we were done praying we would thank God Mom was here for many years to come. I didn't understand her logic behind it then, but I get it now. Sending out that vibration of gratitude for her being here helped keep her here just a little bit longer.

As time passed Mom held on for as long as she possibly could. She wasn't ever going to give in to cancer. Eventually the doctors informed Mom they did not get all of the cancer by removing her left lung. It had spread to her right lung as well. This was yet another time when her stubbornness paid off. In the beginning the doctors gave mom six months to live; she lived two years.

Those two years flew by. Mom was in and out of the hospital a lot. I was eleven by that point and had just started sixth grade. Summer was over and I was so excited and scared to be starting Jr. High School. I often struggled with the guilt of worrying about my own childish problems or being excited, while Mom was sick. The conflict inside me was depressing.

I learned to never be myself around others. I learned to hide who I really was, a scared little girl who was already grown up. To make others feel better I tried to act like what I thought they expected of a normal child. Inside I couldn't wait for them to be gone so I could be my grown-up self. I also knew I couldn't misbehave, not that I wanted to; if I did it would make Mom worse, or so I thought. I did a lot of pretending. I felt horrible if Mom and I argued, so it didn't happen very often. There just wasn't anything important enough to cause Mom the stress.

School was an escape for me where I could keep my mind busy with meaningless work. But it did not last long. It was just a few weeks into the new school year and Mom was in the hospital. She never told me she was going into the hospital for more tests. I came home from school one day and Cindy was at home waiting for me. Cindy told me to get ready because we had to go see Mom at the hospital. Cindy is seven years older than me and loved to boss me around. However this time I could tell she was not just ordering me to do something, she was serious. I did what she said without even asking why.

Cindy and I arrived at the hospital and I was so happy to see Mom. I wanted to cry because she was not at home. Instead I acted like it didn't bother me. I did not want to have Mom worrying about me and get any worse then she already was. My amateur act didn't fool her though. All she had to do was look into my eyes and know exactly what I was feeling. I think for the first time, when I looked into her eyes, something inside me knew this was more than just test at the hospital. There was a sense of despair about her. She hid it well in her attitude and the way she played it off, as if it was just test, but I looked into her eyes and something inside me felt bad.

This was another one of those times when so much was going on, yet nobody would explain to me what was happening. Not knowing what was going on, I thought maybe Mom's despair was just my own imagination. Or maybe that she just didn't want to be in the hospital anymore. I thought this time would be just like the times before when Mom went in to the hospital and would be home in a couple of days. This time was different though. Mom was put into a coma. I am guessing it was done while I was at school. There were no last goodbyes, there were no last "I love you," no chance to say all the things that should have been said.

It wasn't until I was in my late twenties that my sister Cindy told me the coma was induced by the doctors so Mom wouldn't be in pain anymore. As a child I had thought Mom went into the coma because she was sick. I felt betrayed by everyone around me. Why couldn't they have just told me the truth, then? I was as grown up as they were, if not more. I had been taking care of Mom and I was old enough to do that. But instead they just let me find out and piece everything together myself because they just didn't know what to say.

The suddenness of her loss was striking, surreal. One day I had gone in to see Mom at the hospital and she was up talking, smiling and asking me how school was going. The next day she was laying there unconscious, with a tube replacing that luminous smile of hers. It was the first time she ever looked to me like she was losing. When everyone left the room I would talk to her, hoping she would wake up. I told her how much I loved her, I begged her to stay with me and to wake up. I promised I would do everything I could to make her better if she could just wake up. I knew if anyone could wake her it would be me, but I just wasn't enough to keep her here anymore.

Chapter 5

Innocence Lost

"Whether you've seen angels floating around your bedroom or just found a ray of hope at a lonely moment, choosing to believe that something unseen is caring for you can be a life-shifting exercise."
[Martha Beck]

The knowledge that Mom was not going to wake up, ever, finally dawned on me. It became obvious as I observed and listened to all of the people who kept coming to see her. No one ever informed me of Mom's situation, the whispers and talk about what was going on from others were the only clues I got. One advantage to being a child is that I was practically invisible. Most everyone would talk about things without even realizing I was there. One disadvantage of being so young was that no one knew how to tell me or what to tell me.

I remember Deb taking me to the cafeteria at the hospital at one point, but I don't remember what she said to me. I just remember it seemed as if she couldn't find words and she cried a lot. But anything she could have said wasn't anything I hadn't already figured out on my own.

Cindy and I had spent a couple of nights in one of the dark, quiet, yet tiny, family rooms at the hospital. There was a small table and a couple of chairs and a couch that doubled as a bed. It was right near Mom's room. I wanted to make that tiny little room mine forever, for as long as it would allow me to stay near to Mom. I knew we could not stay there forever, but I was hoping no one would actually say that we couldn't. The slightest shred of hope that we could be close to Mom forever in that tiny room was the only hope I had then, and I clung to it desperately. And then the dreaded words came from Cindy's mouth like a dagger stabbing at my heart. "We are going to go home and stay there tonight."

Most kids, at the age of eleven, are worried about not getting what they want. I was too, I guess. All I wanted was for this nightmare to end. I wanted Mom to go home with us. If she couldn't, then I wanted to stay where she was. Screaming and stomping was not going to get me what I wanted this time so when the time came to leave the hospital, I didn't even try to resist. And still, my lack of resistance and lack of knowledge of what to do in that situation, though it seemed the obedient thing to do, has some side effects. As much now as was the case then, my mind would never shut up. It learned to go a thousand miles an hour so that it never stopped long enough to think about what was really going on. It never stopped long enough to recognize how much I was not in control of what was happening to me. My mind already knew how to do this from other negative situations in my world. However, what was happening with Mom made the noise of my fast-moving mind grow stronger and louder than it had ever been before. The noise was a comfort, really. It created a numbness for my pain.

Before we deserted Mom there at the hospital, at least it felt like a desertion, I had a conversation that changed my life forever. It was a conversation where I sat and did the listening while someone else talked. There are a lot of those types of conversations when you are eleven years old.

There was one last thing I had to do for Mom, I was told. This mission was given to me by Mom's favorite preacher who had come to see her that day. After he was done seeing her, he asked Cindy and me to sit down with him at a tiny table in the small, dark hospital room I had been calling home. The light was dim and it felt very much like being in church with the preacher there. This preacher was an older man with a head full of silver-white hair. He had a way with his voice that made you listen, even if you did not want to. In his large hands he held a black leather covered Bible. He seemed to hang on to the Bible like it was his lucky charm.

"You guys must pray to God and tell him to take your mother home. Your mother is hanging on because of you kids." In a stern tone the preacher repeated what he had just said, making sure we got the message. "It is your duty to pray to God and tell him to take your Mother home."

I do not remember much of what else the preacher said that day, but those words echoed in my mind. After listening to the preacher, I felt like the weight of the world was on my shoulders. I trusted in the preacher and knew he was the authority on God, living and even dying. But would it really work to pray to God and ask him to take Mom? Deep down inside I doubted the power of prayer. I also doubted the fact that God would listen to me. He had not listened to me so far when I had asked repeatedly for Mom to be well again.

That one conversation with our preacher shaped my beliefs in God forever. I went home that night and lay in bed and went back and forth in my mind about what the preacher had said to Cindy and me. I decided it was my duty, just like the preacher said, and finally, I did pray. "I don't want Mommy in pain anymore. Please, just take her so she can feel better." I lied to God and told him that I would be alright without Mom. God had to have known I was lying, he is God after all, and yet I knew he would not punish me for lying because I was not doing it for myself, I was doing it for Mom.

I had a very hard time sleeping that night. Things just really felt eerie to me. In 11 year-old terms as I lay in bed, it felt as though I couldn't and shouldn't leave my bed because there was someone under it, though lying in bed unable to sleep was equally torturous. Or, it felt like someone was there watching me, even though I knew no one was.

I was not completely alone because Cindy was there. She had gone to bed right away, as soon as we'd arrived back home. Even with the noise from the TV which I had pushed over to where I could see from my bed, the house felt so empty. It felt lonely and dark because I knew Mom was not there for me to rub her back or make her feel better, like I had done hundreds of times before. I laid there wondering if God heard me. Mom always said, "God answers you, no matter what." One time I had asked, "Mom, why didn't God answer our prayers for you to get better?" Mom just said, "Everything happens for a reason, but God always knows why and He always answers." She even told me we shouldn't question God's answer because He is the only one who knows why.

I tossed and turned that night, wishing I was with Mom. I laid in bed going over what I had said to God. I wondered if God even heard me. I secretly hoped He had not. If He had heard me, how long would it take before He took her home? Everything seemed to take a long time to me at that age, and I figured this would too.

As I laid there in the insanity of my solitude, there were times I would feel the warm tickle of the tears running down the sides of my face into my ears. I knew that Mom was never coming back. I knew I was alone forever. At about three in the morning while I was still awake, the phone rang.

When I heard it, my heart jumped out of my chest. I couldn't answer the phone. It just kept ringing and ringing. Finally I went as far to unplug it, so as to silence this ringing bearer of bad news. I sat down on the edge of my bed for a couple of minutes and argued with myself about plugging the phone back in. Finally, I won.

Slowly I walked towards the phone cord which was barely unplugged from its outlet. Holding my breath I pushed the cord end back into the phone. "RING"! I jumped about ten feet in the air when the phone rang before my fingers were even off the cord. This situation was where I picked up my limited belief about talking on the phone. Logically, I know not all phone calls are bad, but something inside me always says, "Stop. Don't answer that. It's going to be bad news." Even to this day, I still sometimes get a lump in my throat and lots of anxiety when I try to talk on the phone. Even though I have done a lot of work on this issue, it still bothers me. I think when a limited belief becomes this irrational and hard to transform, it becomes a phobia. Thank God for texting!

I picked the phone up and with the sleepiest voice I could use said, "Hello." It was my brother-in-law Curt. "Get Cindy on the phone right now," he said firmly, but not firmly enough to stop me from asking, "Is it Mom?" He replied only by saying, "Just get Cindy on the phone now!"

Knowing Curt was not going to give me any information I ran upstairs and got my sister. It felt like I couldn't move fast enough. Life felt surreal. I started to cry and started to wonder what the hell I had done by asking God to take Mom home. Mom was gone and I knew it, without even needing to be told, and it was entirely my fault. I had prayed and told God to take her home and He had done it. At eleven, I did not know my prayer was going to have such an effect on what would happen. God had answered me. God, in his greatness and power, waited for little me, Miss Eleven-year-old-nobody from Nowhere-ville to give Him the okay to take Mom home.

This was the first time I realized it does not matter to God who you are, He listens and He is there. God doesn't care if you have money, or don't; if you are living on the street broken and poor, or not. He doesn't care if you have a hundred years of life experience, or if you are an eleven year old little girl. I learned as long as you were willing to ask for something, God is willing to give it to you.

Why had God not answered my prayers for Mom to be healthy? It was not what I needed and it was not what Mom needed. Mom's life had been full of purpose and reason. One of the reasons for her life was to teach me something through her death. I had to learn the lesson of what it felt like to lose something as precious and important as my own mother. I had to learn that I never wanted to experience that pain again. I had to have that determination and my newly acquired belief in God to survive my future.

Cindy didn't tell me Mom was gone; she must have known that somehow I already knew. I was already crying before Cindy had even gotten on the phone with Curt and when she hung up, she looked at me and told me to stop crying. So I did; right then and there, I stopped. Curt came over right away to pick us up. In his gentle voice he told me it was okay to cry. But by then, I didn't want to anymore. Instead, I wanted to punch Cindy for having been so insensitive, but I didn't because I felt bad for her. Cindy probably would have just hit me back and who would I tell? Mom wasn't around to run and hide behind anymore.

Cindy and I hurried to get dressed and we all left for the hospital. It seemed to take forever to get to there. Time was moving in slow motion. Mom's room looked different then, compared to all the other times we had been there. Now the room was really clean and there was a soft light on over the head of her bed.

Mom laid there on her back with her eyes closed. She was tucked perfectly in under her bedding. She had been freed from the tube down her throat, as well as all the wires and the IV she had been attached to. She looked peaceful, but also kind of mad. It was as if she knew she was gone and she was pissed off about it. I just continued to stand there, waiting for Mom to move. I stared at her chest and watched for her to take one of her struggling painful breaths. My feet were stuck to the floor and my eyes were glued on her. Everything still felt unreal; I felt like it was not my Mom lying there at all. Could they have replaced her with a look alike?

I wanted to run away, but my damn feet were stuck to the floor. I just kept standing there until someone told me I had to leave. It was as if the words, "It's time to go," had some kind of magical power. Those words released me from being trapped there. Physically I was able to move, but mentally a big part of me is still stuck to that floor in that hospital room, just staring at Mom and waiting for her to move. That day, if they would have let me, I would have laid next to her, like a little bear cub with its mama. I would have buried myself underneath her, curled up in the security of knowing I was done with everything. I would have fallen asleep until my body withered away and died.

But, that was not what I had planned for my life. My life was going to mean so much more than being defined by this moment. Something beyond me allowed me to move on that day and keep living.

Mom passed away on September 11th 1987. This was the day I was orphaned. I was physically alone, left to fend for myself against a cold harsh world, a world which had no sympathy for what I had gone through. That was the day I decided the only one who could tell me what to do anymore was me.

I could not cry because the tears just would not come out. My body and mind were in shock. If Mom had been there she would have asked me why I was feeling sorry for myself. She would have told me whatever doesn't kill you will make you stronger. She would have said, "Don't question it; everything happens for a reason." But part of me did die that day, right there next to Mom. My heart still beat, my body still moved and breathed, but that tiny bit of innocence I had left died that day.

How do you begin to heal from something like this? As a child, you don't; you can't do it on your own. I believe there are things we don't see in this world that help us along and keep us safe until we arrive at a time when we are ready and able to see what it is that we need to do. Some may believe these things are just energy, or our higher selves. Maybe its science or maybe its biblical. Whatever it is, these things are called Angels. They lift you up and help you along until you are able to see the reasons for everything. They carry you without you even knowing it and they get you to where you need to go. They are how I survived during the difficult times. They exist and are as real as anything and everything else because I believe they exist. If you believe that is great! If you think you don't believe you are wrong. If there wasn't a small part of you that believes then you wouldn't be able to even see my words. You wouldn't have created me to write this book.

Chapter 6

Letting Go

"Forgiving does not erase the bitter past. A healed memory is not a deleted memory. Instead, forgiving what we cannot forget creates a new way to remember. We change the memory of our past into a hope for our future."
[Lewis B. Smedes]

Before Mom left this world she had made arrangements for me to stay with my best friend from school, Mendy, and her parents. Mendy's parents are very kind, loving people who always had children around, whether it was their own or foster kids. They agreed to take me in and raise me. They were your picture-perfect parents. Mom's favorite part about them was the fact that I would have the opportunity to go to church every Sunday. I can remember the smile on Mom's face as she would talk about how much she liked Mendy's Mom and how wonderful she thought it was they went to church every Sunday. She knew they would take care of me and I would have a good childhood. Mendy's mom reminded me so much of my own mother and her dad was the father that I had always wanted.

I met Mendy for the first time on the first day of fifth grade, a little over a year before Mom passed away. I had just turned ten the summer before school started and Mendy had turned eleven. The prior year of my life had consisted of watching Mom be sick and spending as much time with her as I could, but I had still been alone quite a bit when she was at work or with Francis. To have met Mendy at that point in my life had to have been completely set up by someone or something who knew I was going to need a friend. Mendy was standing up against the brick wall of the tiny little elementary school the first time I saw her. Mom always told me if I met someone with a smile it was a good sign that they could become a good friend and that was exactly how it happened with Mendy.

She was new to our school and I was curious about her. I saw her standing up against the wall all alone. My first impression about her was she looked kind of mean. But then, as if something nudged me from behind and whispered in my ear, "Go talk to her," I wasn't put off by my first impression. Before I even realized it, I was standing in front of her and introducing myself with a dopey smile on my face. From that day forward, Mendy and I were attached at the hip. We did everything together. I had spent a lot of time at her house and she at mine. When we were playing and having fun I did not have to think about anything except just being a kid. I knew Mom found a lot of comfort knowing I had Mendy and her family around me. It took a lot of weight off Mom's shoulders to know Mendy's family treated me like I belonged there. Her sisters picked on me like I was one of them. Most importantly they loved and cared for me not because they had to, but because they wanted to. That is a feeling sometimes you don't find, even with a real family.

It was as if Mendy's family was planned into my life's path like it was written into my life script. Sometimes I try to imagine what the script looks like. Maybe it would look something like this: Act 1 Scene 2, Julie meets Mendy in the school yard because she is going to need a best friend and new family.

After Mom passed away and after finding out I was going to live with Mendy's family, I took some comfort in knowing that, by being surrounded by people I knew and was comfortable with, things wouldn't have to feel as though they had changed all that much, even though they had. I could pretend I was just spending the night at Mendy's house, like I had done so many times before, except that the sleepovers would never end I would not be able to go home the next day.

Deb had a different idea of where I should be living though. She had been dealing with Mom's passing in her own way. She missed Mom and I am sure that is why she decided she knew what was best for me. I went to stay with Mendy as soon as Mom had passed away. I was at my new home for just a day or so when Deb decided to come to pick me up to spend some time with her. I did not want to go with her, but I had to.

When we reached Deb's house I got a strange feeling I was not there for a play date. Kenny was there too. Maybe Deb thought if Kenny was there to convince me I wouldn't put up much of a fight. She had strategically picked every word, she said, to make me feel as bad as I possibly could about my decision to live with Mendy. I knew where I wanted to live and I tried to explain to her why. I wanted her to know it was not that I wanted to leave my family; I just wanted to be someplace familiar, a place that was already part of my everyday life and a place where for once I might feel a little bit normal. She did not want to listen to me. Deb wanted me to come live with her because she thought I should stay in the family. I felt like a family heirloom that was being passed down. I thought I knew what the consequences would be if I did not agree to live with Deb. My eleven year-old mind did not understand the legalities of the situation, but still I suspected that Deb would take Mendy's parents to court and Deb would win anyway. I didn't want to be a burden to Mendy's parents and actually, this was the first time I experienced feeling like a burden to those around me after Mom passed away.

It is a strong debilitating belief to pick up. All of a sudden you don't feel like you have a right to be where you believe you belong. I suddenly felt like a nuisance in the world because the one person I belonged with was now gone. I felt like owed everyone around me, so I had to do what they wanted so as not to be a burden or cause them any trouble. I started doing anything anyone wanted me to do so that I wouldn't be so noticeable. But it didn't matter how much I tried to please everyone; despite what I wanted, I still felt like I owed everyone.

Eventually, the weight of feeling like a burden wore me down. I could no longer resist feeling like I was a burden to Mendy and her family, so I agreed to go live with Deb and Curt. When I heard myself agreeing, purposefully removing myself from the love and protection of Mendy's family, I knew I was on my own from that point forward. I was going to have to fight my own battles. World: one; Julie: zero, if you want to keep score that is. I felt weak, like I had lost the first round of the endurance test. Another outcome of this choice was that I learned how happy I could make someone by agreeing to do something I did not want to. I learned to sacrifice my own happiness to ease the pain of others. In this situation, I knew how bad Deb was hurting because I was hurting too, and I felt like it was my obligation to take care of my sister's pain by putting my own ideas and feelings aside. I am sure Deb didn't want me unhappy, but I was. Life was depressing and I gave away the last thing that was familiar to me, the last piece of home I had left.

It was not that I did not want to know Deb or be around her. She is sixteen years older than me and was not raised by Mom and she wasn't around much when I was little. As Deb got older, she and Mom never really got along until Mom became sick. However despite any good intentions I had, I just knew our personalities were going to clash. It was so clear to me; I do not understand why she could not see it. Oil and water would have a better chance of getting along then we did. I knew it was going to be a constant battle between us. Even at such a young age, I acted and thought just like Mom. I knew from watching Deb and Mom over the years that there was no way she and I could live together.

Deb had gotten her way and I felt like the world was ending. Even Mom's opinion did not matter. The last decision Mom had made was for me was to stay with Mendy and her family, and Deb did not let Mom have that. She knew living with her was the only way I could stay in the family, especially since Kenny was going off to the Navy and everyone thought Cindy was too young to care for me. That meant Deb was the only other choice I had.

I went to stay with her right away and she wasted no time letting me know who was boss. "You are not allowed to talk to or see Mendy and her family anymore," she told me. This harshness from Deb was, I think, a desperate attempt to feel as though she was controlling the situation and preventing me from changing my mind about willingly coming to live with her. However, it did nothing to earn my trust. I was devastated and wanted to leave right then. Those words just made me hate my sister. I felt like a wild animal being held against its will, trapped in a cage. I could not believe that she was going to take away my best friend after everything I had already gone through. And, she took away my backdoor escape by preventing me from having any opportunity to go back and beg for a spot in Mendy's family again. My good intentions to make Deb happy and feel a little less pain dissolved when she said those words to me. I didn't care about her anymore because she didn't care about me.

I decided to make her life as miserable as possible. Even picking out an outfit for Mom's funeral was a struggle. I wanted something dark and sad she made me wear the ugliest white long skirt and happy, light colored top. If she said something was right, I said it was wrong. I did everything in my power to let her know that I was not happy there. It never mattered though because she was always right and I was always wrong.

The day of Mom's funeral finally came and there was Mom again. I knew it was just her empty shell, but I couldn't wait to see her. I waited until there was no one around the casket, and then I quickly closed my eyes and kissed her forehead. I kissed her hoping that she would wake up. The body that lay in the casket didn't feel like Mom at all; it was cold and fake. Mom had always been warm, soft and cushy, just like a mom should feel. I took one last look at Mom and knew I would never see her again. The world as I knew it was over. It was so dark and gloomy the day of Mom's funeral, of course. Funerals for the people we love always are. The rain fell on and off all day. I pretended the rain was God's tears. God was crying for me because my tears still would not flow. I felt bad I was not crying like everyone else. No matter how hard I tried, I could not make myself cry. I was the saddest person there and I did not have one tear to show for it.

The rain subsided just in time for the burial. During the funeral one of my mom's friends came up to me to give her sympathy. "I am so sorry you lost your mom," she said. I just looked at her and said, "I did not lose my mom, I know where she is." I thought to myself, *why would she say Mom is lost, doesn't this woman know about heaven?* She didn't respond, just handed me ten dollars and walked away. What was money going to do for me? I did not want pity money. I had the urge to find a fire place and throw that ten dollars into it and watch it burn, just like I had watch Vern do when I was little. I know the old lady meant well, but did she really think that money was going to make me feel any better?

After Mom's funeral the nightmares started. I had dreams of her being alive. She would tell me she had to go away because she was a part of some government plan and nobody could ever see her again. In some of my nightmares she would tell me she had witnessed a horrible murder and they had to put her in the witness protection program. I even had one nightmare where Mom was lying in her casket and as I approached the casket, she sat up and started to laugh. She told me it was a joke and she was fine. What cruel tricks the human mind can play on us sometimes.

After a few months the nightmares stopped and eventually turned to dreams. In those dreams Mom would be doing things she did all the time, like getting ready to go someplace special or just being around the house. I would tell Mom how much I missed her. I showed her all the things that had happened since she left. Mom never said anything in my dreams, but I could tell she missed being here with us, too. After dreaming about Mom I would awake to a feeling of emptiness. The dreams did not last long or come very often and I am sure it is because of the disappointment I would feel when I woke up.

I don't know what I miss more, Mom physically being here or what could have been if Mom was here. Of course I miss her hugs and the comfort of her being here, walking through the door after work. Even more, I miss her when I think how my life would be different. I miss knowing if Mom is proud of me. I never got to see Mom hold or love her grandchildren. Sometimes I look at them and I know they would have had their grandma wrapped around their finger. She would have been a wonderful grandmother.

Deb finalized Mom's passing by moving all of my things out of our old house. She packed all of my things into her car. Back and forth we went, between her house and our house. Before I knew it our house was an empty shell, just like Mom had been at her funeral. My whole world was taken away from me and everything I had ever known was gone in one evening. There was no more Mom, house, room, and neighborhood. It was all gone in one second, or at least that's how it felt. Nothing had ever really been mine, now that I think about it. The person those things had belonged to was gone, too. I often found my mind going back to the time when Mom had said, "As long as we are together, wherever we go, will be home." Now that Mom was gone, it didn't matter where I was, I could never call any place home again. In the aftermath of Mom's passing, I picked up the limited beliefs that nothing is mine and that I shouldn't get too happy because it could all be taken away. These beliefs set me up for a life of never being able to settle into one place for long. Until recently, I have had a hard time even putting pictures up on the walls.

Once all the moving was done, I had nothing else to occupy me and was left with only my thoughts. I thought about everything from what I was going to do next, to ending my misery and going to be with Mom. I really did not want to be alive anymore. Mom was gone and everything thing else was too. I had to make a decision. I could take the chicken way out and end it all, or I could continue on and face this world alone. To tell the truth, the only thing that kept me alive was the idea that if I made it to be with Mom in heaven, she would be furious that I was there. Even though she was not physically there in front of me, I could still see "the look" on her face, the look I was sure she would give me if I was to show up in heaven prematurely. There was one thing in this world, or any world for that matter, you did not want to experience and it was "the look" Mom gave when she was pissed! The thought of it is what kept me here.

I promised myself that I would never blame God for anything that had happen to me. I know that Mom, being a very religious person, would have wanted it that way. I figured if Mom could have faith in God with all she had been through, then I could too. It wasn't just for

Mom that I made that promise either. I did it for me. I knew I needed all the help I could get. I knew it was not God's fault Mom died. It always stuck in my mind that everything happens for a reason.

Making this promise to never blame God didn't make things instantly easier. In some sense it made life harder. There was no one to blame for what had happened. It didn't take away the pain of everything. No one had any idea of the torment going on in my mind. I felt so alone and no one in my life could have understood how the aching pain in my heart felt, like an unwanted guest that just would not leave. However, as was the case with many limited beliefs that were being created during this delicate time in my life, the decision to not blame anyone opened my mind and heart for a special kind of help. When things are so bad you just want to give up, but you somehow know there is more than you, let go and let God. This help comes from having faith and a knowing that there is something beyond yourself, even though it's something you can't physically see.

Chapter 7

I Was Never Really Alone

"Angels are all around us, all the time, in the very air we breathe."
[Eileen Elias Freeman]

Deb and I were at war. We chose unusual battlegrounds – my wardrobe, the dining table – but our struggle was as real and painful as if we were in full armor and wielding swords. At times I felt very alone, abandoned even, and mine were circumstances that even a full-grown, mature adult would have had difficulty with. In time, I have been able to look back and make some sense of this period of my life and I marvel out how far I've come in my understanding of the fact that, despite how things felt, I was never really alone at that time. My beliefs in God and the angels that surround us have been created and strengthened to support my memory of this tumultuous time and to carry me forward.

As an example of the many battles I had with Deb, I realized very quickly that she would not listen to me on any subject. For my part, I could not have cared less about what she thought or what she said. It was like Deb wanted me to be four years old again and I was used to being very independent. I had often stayed by myself while Mom was at work or stayed alone late into the night if she was out with Francis, and Deb wanted to treat me like I was incapable of taking care of myself. Deb thought it was wrong for me to stay by myself and found me a babysitter for when she was gone. I liked being by myself because it was the only thing that made me feel like my normal self before Mom got sick. It felt right to be alone.

Deb was also strict on what I could eat. All she wanted me to eat was salads and healthy food, never any junk food like I was used to. She limited me to very small portions and even chose when I could eat. I know it was probably a healthier way, but I didn't care. If Mom wasn't cooking me a four course dinner of steak and potatoes, then I was throwing a frozen pizza in the oven. I ate what tasted good and that was pretty much everything. I ate when I was hungry and that was all the time. It seemed to make Deb happy and proud when I lost a few pounds, but I felt better eating what I wanted, when I wanted.

Food went from being my comfort and my joy to being the enemy. It was something that made me feel so much better even though I was being told it was bad for me, but it was just one more thing in my life I wasn't allowed to have. I began to feel like I was doing something wrong every time I even thought about food. I learned to be ashamed of my addiction to food and my need for freedom in my food choices. My brother-in-law would sneak ice cream smothered in chocolate syrup to me sometimes; he must have felt bad for me. Even though he smuggled me ice cream right before bed, I still lost weight.

My brother-in-law, Curt, is just about the coolest person you could ever meet. He is rustic, humorous and had a great love for his Camaro. When Mom was still alive, Curt would come to see us even if Deb wouldn't. I loved when he came over. He would always joke around and play games with us. He was the one and only person in Deb's house that even came close to being familiar to me. But he was strict too, probably because he didn't want to disappoint Mom or Deb.

It wasn't long before I felt myself breaking out of the cocoon of being a little girl. Instead of becoming a nice butterfly, I started to turn into a rebellious teenager. I even started smoking. Maybe I hoped smoking would kill me. I was twelve and it was cool and bad. I knew it all, in a world of people who knew nothing. I felt mad at everyone and everything because I was hurting. It was easier just to be alone, but even then I had to be alone with myself, and I hated myself. I hated the way my mind just wouldn't be quiet. I

50

was definitely going to need all the help I could get. Somehow I had survived one of the worst things a little girl could have to face, but I wasn't surviving with much grace or ease. Everything in my life at that time felt difficult.

I know now that I was never really alone. So many times I was carried by a force greater than anything I could have comprehended at the time. I was being helped along by my angels. I truly believe, and belief is all that counts in this world, we are just here to contribute our experience to the whole. Everything I had just gone through and experienced was unique to me and I signed up for it; it all is my responsibility to learn my lessons. Fortunately, along with the heartache and pain we write into our contracts, we also write in a time to be helped.

My contract with my Mother looks something like this...

Two women sit down at a table. They are very similar in spirit and soul. The wiser of the women speaks and says, "Here I hold our contract and in it you will find we will both be hurt and feel many heartaches. We both have lessons to learn from each other and I want you to know that only a love as great as ours can survive this kind of experience." Then the younger woman asks, "Why should we go through this kind of pain?" The wiser woman replies, "We will do it for the experience and it will have a reason. You will know this reason when it happens and everything will be understood. You will not have an easy life, but you have to promise me that you will endure it all and no matter how much pain there is, you will finish what you have started."

The younger woman says with some hesitation, "I promise, but I am scared. I have read the contract and you expect me to do this alone!" The wise woman replies, "My dear, you will never be alone, I will always be with you. You see, we are all one and all connected because we are the whole. I may leave the experience to give you the lesson you need, but I am not leaving you because I am you. Whenever you need the knowledge of the whole, it will be there. Whenever there is a situation you cannot handle, we will come carry you until you can. We will watch and whisper to you what you need to hear. Whatever you need comes through a special language called vibration. You don't need to learn the language; it's already there inside of you. The whole is made up of everyone and everything, including guides called angels. I will be one of these guides and can help you through your experience. You are never alone; there are as many angels as you need because they come from within you, for you are part of the whole. Pay attention in the physical world because we will remind you we are there by sending a song or symbols and numbers. We will feel familiar and you will know somewhere deep down who we are. Now go and be born into your experience so we can meet again!"

This contract may be imaginary, but the lesson behind it is real. I have known for a very long time my mother never really left me. She has always been by my side. Even if it is just in remembering her words, she is there. My mom taught me more in eleven years than most people learn in a lifetime. But she continued to teach me even after her death. To me, having an angel around has just become normal and I never have questioned it because I have never known anything different. Just like the contract says, there are certain things I see, hear and feel that remind me I have guides. Everyone does, you just have to pay attention and know how to recognize when things have been conveniently orchestrated. Don't explain it away as just coincidence; give angels their dues and be grateful to them for their help. Your gratitude will bring them closer to you.

My deeper understanding of angels and their role in our existence didn't come upon me overnight. In fact, at eleven years old my understanding of God, angels and the universe in general was very naïve. It was exactly what I needed to believe at the time because it was an incomplete understanding, and it prompted me to search deeper for answers and a more thorough grasp on God and the angels. So, it was not wrong to believe the way I did at the time, as a young girl. It was the way my child mind could comprehend the world I was creating.

Back then, to me God was the creator of the world as I knew it. God was to be feared and, much like parents, He did things to us to teach us lessons even if those lessons were hard. Basically He was a man who lived in the clouds in heaven and watched over everything and decided what happened to us. God sat at His desk on a cloud somewhere waiting for us to ask things of Him through prayer. Prayers were like a cordless phone straight to God. Angels were people who received their wings as a reward for their good deeds and selfless acts. Angels were there to carry out God's orders. The universe was a place which consisted of the earth, all the planets, stars and anything else beyond the blackness and nothingness of where it all existed. Everything was separate from me and all things were separate from one another. Those were my beliefs for a very long time, even well into my adulthood, only changing slightly. I didn't question them I just accepted them as fact.

Those ideas might seem a little ridiculous now, but I can tell you without doubt all of it did exist because I believed it did. Each experience is unique to each person because you are creating it as you go. No one is right or wrong as long as they believe. How many arguments and wars would have not happened if people would just agree that all things are possible and can exist at any time and at the same time as long as there is someone there to believe? People have this need to know it all when really the only truth is that we should let go and realize we know nothing. The wonderful thing about beliefs is they will change when you need them too; they are not solid.

God, angels and the Universe have grown into something very unique to me over time. My understanding and experience of all continually changes and becomes enhanced, as long as I keep an open mind. I have a very nice mix of scientific, spiritual, individual beliefs about life. No matter what or how I have believed about world, the thing that has been consistent is how things show up to help me along the way. Now, to me God is still the ring leader and where I place my order and angels still do good deeds, but they are no longer people or unexplained events. Now they are people I have created and events that I have allowed to happen. The universe still contains everything including God and angels, but is no longer something that is separate and outside of myself. The universe is inside me; it is in my heart and in my mind and I am responsible and in control of what happens to me.

This point bears repeating because of its great importance: there is nothing outside of ourselves. Does this exist for me? Yes! Does it for you? Only if you believe and it feels true to you. What you believe right now in this very moment is what is real. I know it is unusual to say this, but I am going to tell you something you need to hear: You are right! Even if you think everything I say here is wrong, you are right. Within each person exists their own universe. So, if you are looking for instruction and guidance in the words that I write, I can only tell you this... Everything here in all of my books is mine and it is 100% real, because I believe it. If you also believe it, it can be 100% real to you as well. If you disagree with my beliefs, *you are right* – for you – and your disagreement doesn't make my beliefs anything less than 100% real, *for me*.

You find yourself reading what I have written because something in you is ready for confirmation of what you believe, or you are ready for a change in what you currently believe. You have created me to be what you need in this moment; I am not speaking to your conscious mind, I am writing from your subconscious.

The best part about being part of the whole is that what you need to know or hear as guidance right in this moment is the same thing I need to express and share. There is nothing that you need that isn't ever available to you because it is always a part of you. Even if it is words you need to hear or read, a hug from a friend, kindness of a stranger or even money it is all right there waiting for you to open yourself up to receive.

Although I have had some healing moments I attribute to what I call angels, I have not even begun to heal from my mother's life and death. Although I have a different perspective about why she is gone, that doesn't cure any of the pain or the limited beliefs created by what I was a witness to. I have ignored what needed to really be dealt with for a very long time and as I write this, I realize that only by writing my story have I begun to address what needs to be done. I need to heal and so do you or you wouldn't be reading this. Whenever what I have written here is read, it heals me a little more.

Through my pain and experience I can give to the world my

knowledge. Through my giving lies my healing. I know this because I pay attention to things around me. I look for those signs, symbols and feelings I believe come from my angels. As I began to write this chapter I became blocked. I wanted to write a directory on angels and how to heal with their help. Honestly I didn't know what to write. Even though I have been counting on their help for a very long time, I am not an expert on angels or anything else for that matter. What opens me up to write is my own call for help. This is what I have learned in all my experience. I call out for my angels to help and they come running. They don't stand in front of me and tell me exactly what to do, rather they give me ideas, guidance, inspiration and just somehow I know what to do. Everything just seems to flow.

It is as easy as calling to them, but what I need to share is how I use what they give me and how I ask for what I need. Just like me, you have had things show up in your world when you needed them. If you are not willing to recognize what is going on then you cannot utilize what is being given to you (what you have given yourself).

I am here to give you a different perspective and to change your point of view on how you are creating the world around you all the time, whether or not you realize it. You are ready to receive this different perspective. How do I know this? Because you asked for it; it's why you have been brought to read this book.

Chapter 8

Angels among Us

"He will give his angels charge of you to guard you in all your ways. On their hands they will bear you up, lest you dash your foot against a stone."
[Psalms 91:11-12]

Let me revisit the contract between my mom and I for just a moment. For more information on utilizing the scripting of a contract as a way to frame your life, I refer you to the first book in this series, ***Preacher's Li'l Secret.*** In the contract with my mother, she explained she may leave this earth but that she would still be with me even afterwards. Though it took me some time to realize it, I now know that my mother has been with me ever since the day she died. She is one of my guardian angels. She was my angel when she was here in the physical and now also in the spiritual sense.

As I said, it took me some time to realize this. At first, after her death, the longer I had to go without my Mom physically being here with me the more I felt distant from her. At that point in my life I must have needed that distance from her as I was angry and hurting because I felt she had left me and I didn't understand why. During my teens and my twenties I would try not to even think about her because it hurt so badly. During those dark years, I began to feel like my mom and the life I had once had with her was all a dream. None of my past felt real at all. Many years later there was a moment when I did realize that she had never left my side. When that moment came, I knew without a doubt that my mother was always there, and always had been.

Even when I was ignoring her, my mother was there. I didn't know it then, but she was sending me signs and watching over me, keeping me safe while I made my way towards that moment when I had the realization she was there. She never gave up on me. Mom followed me faithfully and patiently, waiting for me to acknowledge her existence. Looking back at it all now, there were many close calls and instances that brought me to the conclusion that if she had not been my guardian angel, I would not have survived. How I came into my current understanding of angels involved a long process. Being able to have had these experiences is amazing, almost as exciting as being able to share them with others.

What are angels?

There are many kinds of angels in this world – those that guard us and help us through life, like my mother; those that are angels of nature; angels who are warriors that keep us safe from evil; and, of course arch angels, just to name a few. A quick internet search will yield a very through list of all the different types of angels and what their primary roles are.

My goal here is not to reiterate what you can learn very simply from a multitude of sources, but rather to tell you what I have learned for myself through my experiences. As you begin searching for your answers about angels, you'll likely find it fun to learn about all the different types and I encourage you to learn as much as you can and enjoy the education. Just remember, it is not necessary at all to memorize or even know which angel does what and why or even how. The most important thing for you to learn is this: angels do exist and they can hear you!

What do they do?

Angels already know exactly who needs to help you, what it is you need, and where and when you need this help. They will also try to bring this help to you in a way that will make you know it was they who brought it. They really do like to be acknowledged for the assistance they give us, not for the praise and glory of it, but because when you acknowledge what they have done it makes them stronger.

In a sense, acknowledging angels is what keeps them wearing wings. When you acknowledge what they have done it makes your belief in them stronger and more solid. Belief is everything, the most important thing, and if you believe they can help you it makes it a lot easier for them to help you the next time.

A lot of what I say about angels is going to sound familiar to you for a couple of different reasons. The first reason is that I am telling you what you already know. Deep within, you already know everything I am telling you; it just needed to be awakened in you. Your awakening is occurring as you read my words. The second reason this will sound familiar to you is that a lot of what I say about angels will sound like the law of attraction. That is because it is. Angels have a special place in the law of attraction and are the guidance and help of the system. They are there to give you clues and help bring your desires to you, according to what you are attracting. The Law of Attraction is also a topic I discussed in the first book of this series, in case you need to refer back to it.

To get a grasp on the concept and theory and experience of angels, it may help you to think at first about the word 'angels'. When you think of this word, think of it more as an action word, a form of help which carries its own resonance, even giving it a solid form sometimes. This "help" or "angels" can be physical or spiritual, tangible or invisible, depending on their resonance. If you don't believe in God, angels can even be scientific. Again the importance lies in what you personally believe and the peace that comes with knowing that, regardless of what you believe, you are right.

How will I know the Angels in my Life?

The "magic" of angels can be worked through different people, animals or anything physical. Sometimes it doesn't take anything physical, like a person, for things to happen. Angels even work to aid us through ideas, events, thoughts, feelings, intuition, symbols, numbers, even through your senses. The important thing to know is, we must keep an open mind and not have a set of expectations as to how, where and when angels will manifest themselves in our lives.

Specifically related to my mother as an angel, I know there are many ways my mother works her magic. Sometimes I just close my eyes and smell lilacs because it reminds me of giving them to her on Mother's Day. Or sometimes I smell Freedent gum and it reminds me of the way her purse smelled as I rummaged through it for gum on a Sunday morning in church. When I smell that gum I can feel my mother sitting next to me and remember how safe I felt. When I am feeling down, Mom always seems to find a way to get me to hear the song *Lean On Me,* just so I know she is there. She will show me the numbers 911, the date she passed away, if she wants me to pay special attention to something or someone who needs my help. Sometimes the signs of the angels are obvious, sometimes more subtle. Regardless, the closer we pay attention and the more diligent we are at watching for their signs and acknowledging them for their signs, the more our angels will appear to us.

As I said earlier, lay down your expectations and concepts of what you think the manifestations of angels will look like. There are a million ways they make themselves known, in small ways and big, and it will very rarely but what you expect. Angel magic can happen when you feel the wind against your skin on a warm summer day and, for some unknown reason, it makes you smile and feel that life – your life, your life right now – is good. Things can sometimes seem to just happen on their own. In my experience, Mendy was there at school the very day I needed her to be, as if the angels had perfectly scripted our chance meeting. Take advantage of each of these moments and acknowledge the angels for them.

Angels even work towards our greater good through our intuition and feelings. For example, when we begin to get off track from our life's path or when we are doing things that are counterproductive, you can know this by what you are feeling. You will feel bad if you are not paying attention and listening to your guides about where you need to go. In the same way paying attention to the outside signs from your angels is important, so also it is equally important to pay attention to the inner signs such as how you are feeling and your intuitions. I've learned it's important to pay attention to your feelings, even the ones that aren't comfortable. Our feelings are not there not to hurt us, but are our navigation system in this world.

There have been several times when life was so bad and I felt so lost that I didn't recognize the signs or feelings I was being given. Not paying attention to them didn't make them go away, but it made my life so much harder. I became desperate during those moments. Desperation has its purpose in life too. Each time I became drowned in desperation, I learned a little something about myself and what the word desperation really means. Most people see the idea of desperate as a bad thing. I believe it is just a resonance we get into sometimes when we don't know what to do. It becomes a beacon to the angels that we are now in a place where we need their help and will grow from their help.

Just before you reach the point of desperation, you may find yourself in a situation where you feel lost and panicked. It feels as if everything is chaos and you have lost control. You can't imagine, see or understand what you need to do. This feels awful, I know! It is horrible and depressing! I've learned though that it is at these times when we are most resistant to letting go of what we think we need to have control over. When you get to that point where you know all is lost and nothing in this world can make your desire manifest and you give up, it is in that very second you are in desperation.

Desperation is a vibration that resonates out to the universe stating, "I give up! I don't care how it happens anymore; my beliefs, my ideas, my blocks are gone!" You are in what I call the "let go and let God" moment. Your blocks seem to dissolve away and all of a sudden, a miracle happens! When you give up out of desperation, it opens you up to the point of *allowing*. You allow God, angels and the universe to bring you what you desire in the perfect way, in a way your conscious logical mind could not have imagined.

So, remember, desperation is not a bad thing! Essentially, desperation is another safety net we have written into our contracts. It is just another way of manifesting your desires. Although not bad, it can be a painful, difficult, exhausting way of doing things. It most defiantly is *the hard way* of communicating between you, God, the universe and your angels. I'm not saying that the experience of desperation shouldn't happen, because it does and will and it is so valuable in teaching us so much about ourselves. But things can be easier if you are in control of when and how you "let go and let God". That is the only thing you should concern yourself with being in control over. If you just learn to rely on those that are there to help, your life would be so much easier. Have faith it will come.

A Better Way

Instead of being desperate and not knowing how something is going to come to you, angels and miracles give your mind a "how" or a needed explanation. As physical beings we sometimes have a need to be logical and have to be able to explain how things happen, instead of just being happy that they happen. It is not a flaw that we do this. It is because we want to be able to learn and repeat what we have done so that next time it is more efficient. It is awesome that humans work this way and this study of cause and effect that we perform almost without even realizing it is what has allowed us to evolve and create in the physical world. But it can be our block as well. What we need to learn is sometimes things can't be explained or known. If you're anything like me you are still going to want to dissect the situation and have your explanation.

From the very birth of an idea, you can bypass the desperation part of the manifestation process by giving it up to angels to create those miracles for you. You can pacify your conscious mind's needs by giving it the explanation of how these things are going to happen. I know it takes a lot of courage to give up the control of when, where, and how something will happen, and I know it is especially hard to give up that control to something you can't always see. But it does make things so much easier in life. Just remember, essentially you have never given up control because from the beginning you are the one writing the contract. You are just learning to have faith in yourself and know what you have written is what you needed to learn. Take comfort in knowing you would never write a contract for yourself without giving yourself guidance and help. Angels are that loop hole you have written into your contract so you don't have to be alone and you have guidance to make your lessons a little easier to learn. I bet any lawyer would say, "Sounds pretty logical and smart to me!"

Why can't angels just step in and help us from the beginning? It is because of the vibration you are holding onto when you don't let go. That vibration is so dense that it becomes solid. It is like a brick wall that no one, not even an angel, can break through. This is why you may have heard it said, "You have to ask for what you desire when you are trying to manifest." Or you may have heard, "Angels can't mess with free will." Even the Bible says, "Ask, believe and receive." Asking is the first step because it starts to break down that wall of letting go of a need to control and understand. When you are asking or even falling into desperation, you are changing your vibration from someone who does it all and needs no help to a vibration of someone willing to accept help. The brick wall changes and becomes weaker. When the wall is gone, this allows the angel part of you to access the part of you that already contains what you desire. What you desire is already in you. It has just been blocked by your need to control how you have access to it. Angels just go and grab it and show you that it is there. Or sometimes they try to get your attention to show you it has been there all along.

We Still Have Lessons to Learn

There will be times when angels can only carry you through a bad situation instead of making it all better. Angels can't change the lessons you have to learn in life. For example, some of you may look at my childhood story and ask, "How can Julie believe in angels when she had all of these things happen and no one came to help her?" Mom dying, Deb being the way she was and anything else bad that happened didn't happen because of the lack of angel support. Those were the times which I had written into my contract as lessons I needed to learn from Mom and Deb. During such times, all the angels can do is hold my hand and whisper in my ear, "This too shall pass."

We experience this time and time again in our lives especially when it comes to our children. When we send our children to school for the first time, they fall and scrape their knee, or we take them for their drivers test. We know it is going be painful or difficult and we wish we could take away the pain or have the experience for them, but we push our children to do it anyway.

The best example I can give happened just recently. My daughter was selling Girl Scout cookies at a cookie booth set up by her troop. When we first started selling that day, both my daughter and one of the other little girls were nervous to ask people to buy cookies. I would stand behind my daughter and nudge her out toward people as they walked by to encourage her to ask. I admit every time my daughter would ask, I would cringe at the idea of someone telling her no. By the end of the day she had made many sales and it had become very easy for her to ask. We were even having fun with it and my daughter would have liked to have stayed longer. On the way home, my eight year-old daughter gave me an insight that made me so proud of her and proud of myself. She said, "Mommy, whenever someone walked by us you pushed me and told me to ask, but the other girl's mom grabbed her daughter and pulled her daughter towards her when people walked by!" Then my daughter looked at me and smiled and said, "Mommy, I feel good about myself and I wonder if the other girl does." That day I gave my daughter courage and her self-esteem was through the roof. Just like a parent, our angels will stand behind us, making sure we don't get hurt too bad, but will refrain from taking away our lessons. They will not interfere in your experience. That is how important the experience is.

Everything you have just read is my version of how angels exist in my universe. Beliefs are specific to each person and they are the part of you that creates your world. At this point, I invite you to go above and beyond your beliefs to come up with your own thoughts and ideas about what angels are and what they can do for you and what they have done for you. You are only limited by your imagination! The possibilities are endless. Just like I did with my daughter that day, I am going to push you to break through your limits. You are not bound or tied to what is already in this world. If you want to create something mystical and magical in your world to help you heal or to give you what you desire, then go ahead create it! The power to do so already lays waiting inside of you. You can even ask your angels to help point it out.

Chapter 9

A Guide to Creating Your Guides

"Close your eyes and feel the brilliance within. It's there,
waiting for you to notice. You are enough. You are brilliant.
You are guided."
[Elena Lipson]

Guides are an important part of finding our way through our life's journey and guiding us is an intrinsic element of the help we can choose to be open to receiving from the angels. There are no right and wrong answers when it comes to how you will be guided though, and many people become discouraged early on when the guides in place for one person don't manifest the same way for them. So, it's essential that you realize your guides are what you create them to be.

In this chapter I am going to help you expand your ideas so you can become open to the endless possibilities that exist as you begin creating your guides. Like a box of hundreds of shades of colored pencils, there are ideas for shades of ideas you may never have thought of for yourself until you see an example of it and think, "Yes, I like that color, I'm going to choose it for myself." The essential ingredient you will need in creating your guides is a simple, yet powerful, thing indeed. That is, the ability to ask questions and more importantly, ask the right questions.

Why are questions so important? I personally think asking questions is a tool given to us so we can figure everything out just a little faster and get to our life lessons *a lot* faster. Children are a perfect example of this. As children, one of the first things we do when we begin learn and are able to speak is to ask questions – a lot of them! – because it is an instinctual and natural to want to learn. Usually children ask simple questions, like "why?" However I think the word "what" is just as important. Starting with a "why" or "what," sometimes "how," is a good place to begin simply because those one word questions tend to grow into bigger questions. We should each take a lesson from the child-version of ourselves and get back to a simpler place where we asked questions, regularly and frequently.

You might be wondering what the value of questions is in our life's journey. From my experience I have learned that each question we pose to the universe will always result in an answer, at some point. One way or another, there will be an answer, so be on the lookout for it! The answer to your question can come in any way, shape, or form and, at least in my experience, is very often not in any way, shape or form you are expecting or in the timeframe you are expecting. But remember, asking a question to the universe or God or even to your angels will always come back answered because the question itself is attached to you.

If you ask the right question it can take the limitations out of what you are in need of. For example, let's say you ask for a million dollars. There are lots of beliefs around that million dollars and it may not come right away because of those beliefs. Instead of asking, "When can I have a million dollars? I need it!" a better question might be, "Why has a million dollars not come to me?" or "how did the future version of myself get that million dollars?" You will get signs and be shown what life lessons you need to work on to clear yourself of the limited beliefs keeping you from your creation. It's up to you whether or not you will take care of those limited beliefs that are standing between you and that million dollars.

Building on this concept of asking the right questions, let's continue talking about guides by asking some simple questions to make it easier to figure out what kind of guides you need to create. It is important to say that this is only a guide to expand upon, not a one-size-fits-all solution. It is also important to note this is not something you have to do in order for your angels to come to you. They know no such prerequisites and will show up no matter what, as long as you ask for them.

Do you need angels in your life?

Because you are reading this, you probably will answer yes. But there might be some of you who are satisfied with where you're at in your life's journey and not at all paying attention to your angels right now, and that is perfectly fine too. I encourage you to read the rest of the questions anyway as something might pertain to your situation and you might find help in your own ideas about the questions.

My thoughts about this question are, go beyond the yes. I encourage you to over-analyze this and all the questions I give you, and write down whatever comes to mind when you answer each one. When I first answered this question, I answered "yes" and immediately it brought me to another question.

Why?! Or, why might I not need guides?

Of course this could have been the first question, but I didn't want to leave out people who might not want anything to do with their guides. How did I answer this question? I need my angels because without the thought of them being there, I feel alone. I would feel unprotected in this world without the support and help they give me. I am open to the assistance I feel they can give me.

What is it you need help with?

I ask this question daily. Some days the answer is the same as the day before. Sometimes it is a last minute question I ask to help me find a quick answer. Sometimes my answer comes out of being frustrated because the answer that day is something I have been struggling with and I should have asked for help long ago. When you remember to ask this question it is because your guides are whispering in your mind to ask it. They are nudging you forward. This question always brings me to my next question.

What kind of guide or guides do I need?

How much you care to know about angels will determine how much detail you want to put into the characteristic of your guides. Your guides can be as general or complicated as you want them to be. If you have time to read and research and you want to go by someone else's template then that is great. If you want to make all of them up on your own then that is awesome too. My guides are a mixture of some everyone knows and some that are unique to me. You already know I have my mother as a guardian angel and beyond that I also like to think of arch angel Michael and a couple of other ones I rely on that are probably well known. But then I have guides that are made up. For example, when I was going to therapy to deal with some of my issues I was told to picture in my mind's eye some beings to help me get through my own limited beliefs. As soon as I closed my eyes and my therapist began talking, I could picture them. They were beings with their own characteristics, not detailed in how they looked except how large and bright they were. There were four of them and each represented something I needed as a child such as justice, confidence, protection and comfort. I would imagine myself being in the middle of the four beings and when I was ready, I would move into the painful memory my therapy session was focusing on and, in a sense, I would then move forward from it and become unstuck. I found these guides and this method very useful and began to use this technique on my own, outside of therapy.

I found the above method of calling on my angels very easy and have used it a lot. It was particularly helpful a couple years ago when I began physically feeling the effects of not having dealt with my mother's passing. My unresolved issues with my mother's passing began to manifest themselves into a physical illness. I wasn't sure exactly what parts of me were still stuck in the past, but I had avoided it long enough and it was time to deal with it. Since I was not sure exactly which part of this experience with my mother needed my attention the most, I asked for help from the guides I had created with my therapist. I imagined the four beings surrounding me as I walked and when I came to my destination, I realized I was eleven years old. The beings moved from around me and the scene was relived. There I was, stuck in that moment when I was there with my mother in her hospital room right after she had passed.

I felt myself stuck to the floor and my eyes stuck to my mother, waiting and watching to see if she would breathe or move. At the same time I could see myself through the eyes of the beings.

Each one looked at me and knew exactly what I needed to move forward in that moment and say good bye to it. After each one gave me what I needed, my feet were released by the floor and I was free to walk around the room. I walked right up next to my mother and I touched her, I said good bye and I told her I would be fine. I could feel my guides were standing behind me. As I turned around and saw my guides standing with open arms, I could feel myself changing from an eleven year old little girl to a grown woman. As I walked I realized where my guides were leading me. I found myself at the door of my mom's hospital room. The door was open and as I walked through it, I looked back and my mom was no longer in that bed. Just like me, she had moved on.

I can still recall that moment in time when my mother was in that hospital bed, but when I think about it now I never view myself as being in that little girl's mind any longer. I view it from outside of her, as if I am watching from another perspective. I am just an observer. That is an important part of letting go of limited beliefs, realizing you don't just forget it. It is all still a part of something I experience, but I have downloaded that within the memory bank of the universe so now I can move on. I don't need to keep reliving that moment time and time again.

What do you already have?

What are your traits? In my opinion the most important part about creating or becoming familiar with your guides and utilizing their abilities to help you is recognizing what you already have. I consider myself a somewhat humorous person at times and I think laughter is important. So, some other guides I have created are some famous ones. Sometimes I use the idea of what I think Lucille Ball or Chris Farley might tell me if I need someone with a huge sense of humor. Guides don't have to always be someone who has passed, they can be anyone. Your guides can have many characteristics from many different people. Starting with who you are is a good place to begin because they come from you and there is no one as important as you in your universe. Who or what your guides are will also depend on what you need in the moment, such as whether you need a serious angel, a comedic one or one who is smart, like Albert Einstein. Your guides are only limited by your imagination.

How real do you need your angel to be?

I think I have a nice mix of real angels and imaginary ones. Along with the guidance of the beings I created to help me through places I am stuck in, I have also come across some real life ones. The real life ones are created the same way as the imaginary ones and, like real angels, they begin to exist to fill a need you have! You already know how I feel about my mom being an angel, but in addition to my mom I have had a lot of other real angels too. They never really seem to be in my life for very long, sometime just for a few seconds and then they are gone, sometimes longer. But for me none have been physically with me for a very long time. They serve their purpose and then they disappear.

How do you want your angels to help you?

I choose to have my angels help me in mystical and magical ways, such as a stranger with a kind word just when I need to hear it or seeing something unexplainable that makes me know there is more to this world then what I have created. I love discovering all the wonderful ways my angels can help me. I like to come up with my own ways, but I also like to leave it open for anything to happen. This is how paying attention comes in to play when you decide you want your guides to help. If you don't pay attention, you won't discover all the different ways they can help.

How long does it take to create your angels and how much time do you need before they help you?

These questions, like all the others, are based on your beliefs. Do you want everything to happen fast? Do you believe it can? Or do you believe everything happens in the time it is supposed to? Do you think angels function within the constraints of human time constraints? I don't believe they do. It is my belief that they exist in all of time, at the same time. We as humans are the ones that have created time as a way to compare, measure and grade ourselves. If we didn't have time as humans we might forget when it is time to go and we would forever be here on this earth. I believe it is limiting to create guides that must work within the constraints of human-created timelines.

How much time do you think your angels expect of you?

This is one question I have struggled with in the past. I used to have the feeling that if I didn't spend a lot of time recognizing, thinking about and learning about angels, they would not want to spend a lot of time helping me. I have discovered it just simply wasn't true or it just became untrue for me. My angels understand I don't have time to sit around all day learning about what other people's ideas are about them. My angels are already there and know I can't spend all the time in the world creating them either. Understanding and knowing my angels is just as simple as asking and allowing the knowledge. Most of all, as long as there is love for them and gratitude for their help, they are grateful for the opportunity to serve you.

These are just a few questions I think will help you as a general guide and will also help you to create your own questions too. If it is all too fluffy and too much to think about, then don't. The only take home message I have for you is this: your guides will only care about all this as much as you do. Do it all in your time in your way.

Chapter 10

Communicating with Your Guides and Angels

"Insight is better than eyesight when it comes to seeing an angel."
*[Eileen Elias Freeman, **The Angels Little Instruction Book**]*

As in any relationship, communication with your guides and angels is of paramount importance. If you don't communicate, how else will you receive their help and guidance? And yet, communication is a two-way street, isn't it? Your angels and guides will be working to communicate with you too, but what if you aren't prepared to receive and hear their messages? I have found that there are many ways in which we communicate with our angels and guides and I'll be sharing some of those tools with you here. But first, the overarching skill that must be adopted is confidence. Let me explain.

Confidence is the key to communication with your angels. Those in the early stages of learning to walk with their guides and angels, and those who are more experienced, often find confidence lacking. As an example, consider a person who has reached out to their angels to guide them through a tricky spot along their path. As expected, the angels reach out to this soul, giving signs and guidance as requested. The person senses that the signs they are seeing are from their angels, but lacks confidence in the communication. They second-guess themselves; they are unsure of whether a sign they saw was from their angels, or a mere coincidence. The message to them from their angels is lost in this mental shuffle between confidently receiving the signs of the angels and second-guessing themselves. This is not uncommon and so I would like to share a bit with you now about ways in which I have helped the communication between myself and my guides and angels by gaining confidence.

The first thing I struggled with was confidence when I started realizing I had guides. I had a problem with not knowing it all. It was that feeling of lack of information that caused my confidence issue. Now I know this was yet another limited belief I carried. As a result, that limited belief put up blocks so I wouldn't notice when my guides were trying to help me or even when they were trying to communicate. I felt like if I did not do enough research and didn't know the ins and outs of what angels were all about, I couldn't trust the communication I was sensing was real.

My confidence didn't come with more research and learning about angels. My confidence came in having faith in my contract and in myself. Once I transformed my belief about how much I had to know it opened me up to a whole different world. I transformed my belief into something more serving. Now, my confidence comes from this: the universe was never outside of me. Since everything exists within my mind and heart, I already hold all knowledge about everything that ever was or ever will be and it is always accessible to me.

I know it might sound a little arrogant to say I know it all. It may help if I explain a little further. Since everything exists inside my mind and heart, if I desire something, including what I desire to know about angels, I just ask. Whatever I ask starts to manifest and will be shown and come to me in the physical world. This works for anything and everything. What is going on inside will manifest or reflect itself onto the "real" world.

Now that I have opened up more through transforming my beliefs I am free to notice when angels communicate with me. Angels are always trying to communicate through limitless ways. How you communicate with them depends on your beliefs. How they communicate with you will depend on you as well. Each person's experiences with angels and guides is unique to that individual. Here are some thoughts that might help you along your journey as you look for the unique ways in which communication with the angels will manifest in your life.

Tap into Your Knowing

As I mentioned, the knowledge your brain craves as a way of giving you confidence that you know enough to actually receive communication from your angels and guides, already exists within you. Therefore, you need only to tap into your knowing. Ironically, this tapping in is yet another way of communication with your guides.

Try this: Relax. For even just a few moments, exist in a space that is unfettered, that is simple and uncomplicated. Imagine yourself connecting in this space with the superconscious that lies within you. I promise you don't have to be a psychic oracle or a master meditator to see things the way they are or how they are going to be in order to access divine guidance in this way, as it simple exists already inside you.

I have found one of the easiest ways angels communicate is through a knowing. Continue practicing accessing the knowing within and it will begin to come more easily to you. Now, there are times when I have interactions with my guide through tapping into my inner knowing and information will seem to just come to me. I find it quite beautiful to witness this transmission of communication, especially when there is a marked difference in what I already knew and what the angels are showing me in these times.

By writing

A good way to decipher what is you and what is your guides and angels is to write down what you are thinking. You may begin to notice through your writing when ideas don't sound like you. Or you will write in the third person as if someone is talking to you and out from you. There is a mystical connection between our inward knowing and our hand grasping a pen, something that is seldom duplicated when we swap a keyboard and screen for pen and paper. Janet Conner does an amazing job of helping us develop this channel in her book *Writing Down Your Soul*.

When you write, ask a question. Then write down anything that comes to you, even if it doesn't make sense. Writing is a wonderful tool to use. So many great things and ideas come from yourself and from your guides as you write. It makes those ideas more solid and takes them from being just ideas to being more physical and real. It is the first place I recommend you start. Writing is especially helpful in recognizing the ways your angels are communicating. Write down every time you have ideas you think might not have come directly from your mind or that feel outside yourself. You can write down any physical signs too. Giving physical recognition to physical signs lets you notice them more.

Observe the Physical

There are many physical ways in which angels will communicate. One main way they communicate with me is to leave me feathers. When I wrote the first book in this series, ***Preacher's Li'l Secret,*** I struggled with the cover of the book. I felt stuck and struggled with everything I tried. Then I asked for an answer from my guides. Within minutes I came up with an idea. It felt right and I knew what I was doing was right, but still questioned myself. Right before I walked outside to take the picture related to my idea, I asked for confirmation. When I opened the door and went to take the first step down off the porch I looked down and there was a beautiful white feather.

Instances like this, where I ask for confirmation and I see a feather or another sign, happen on a daily basis for me. Feathers are my sign that I am on the right path, but everyone's signs are different and yours will be too. There are things such as movies and songs that angels can use to give you a message or inspiration. You probably have already had a one of those days when you needed to hear certain words and turn on the radio and you hear the perfect song. Pay attention to physical experiences like this.

A few years ago I was going to see a medium. I questioned her abilities and questioned if I was doing the right thing. I asked my Mom for a sign and at 9:11 a song came on the radio; it was ***Lean On Me.*** That song will forever remind me of my mother because it is the only song I can remember hearing her sing. Do things like this exist because I believe they do? You bet. It's that belief that opens me up to see them. Everything exists just waiting there for you to believe.

Angel Cards

You don't have to wait around for signs if you don't want to. Signs from angels are fun to find and you can get them anytime you need them. However there is an easier way. You don't need to be anyone special to use this way. My best advice on how to receive messages from your guides is to use angel cards. You can make up your own or buy some. You can even go online and find websites to get free angel card readings. Whatever way you choose, just simply follow the directions given to use your new tools of communication.

Most angel cards work the same way. You ask a question of your angels and then randomly choose a card. Sometimes I feel guided to choose one card, sometimes three. While the card or cards you choose may be random to you, the cards you select are not random to the angels guiding you. The card revealed to you will provide guidance and clarification related to the question you initially asked and the angels know what you need to see in order to be helped by their guidance.

Angel card answers never fail. Most cards will be a general answer to a question you pose, or might provide insight on a situation you are faced with. For instance, my son was having a problem with bullies at school and he continually asked me not to get involved. It felt wrong as his mother to not interfere and protect him. I was torn between what he wanted and my instincts as a mother. I asked the cards for help. The first card and only card I needed was *See Only Love.* I pondered over what the card meant for some time and I took it as a message from the angels to hold those boys picking on my son in a place of love and understanding in my heart and hold my son there as well.

I asked the angels show me when and if I needed to step in and I asked my angels to protect him while letting him learn his lesson

77

from what was happening. In a very short time I received a message from my older daughter, Alex. She received a message from a girl at my son's school who knew her because Alex is friends with her sister. The message was one of desperation. The girl was a friend of my son and was concerned about him getting bullied. She went to the teachers and asked for help and felt my son was not getting the help he needed. When I heard that someone was reaching out saying my son needed help and the people who should be helping and protecting him weren't doing their job, I was livid. I was shaking inside my skin with anger. I felt I had let my son down and I immediately began planning a trip to the school where I would be irate, scream, yell and defend my son to the people who were supposed to be watching out for him. In my rage, before I did anything, I grabbed my angel cards. I didn't even ask a question, I simply shuffled them as I always do before I pick a card and picked one at random. I flipped it over and, again, the message was *See Only Love*!

It stunned me so much when I received the message again that I stopped and wondered what I was supposed to do! Again I read through the message my daughter had sent me from the girl trying to help my son. There was the name of the counselor who the girl had gone to for help. I took a deep breath and I called the school. The teacher wasn't available but while I waited for a return call, I was able to meditate and concentrate on the wisdom provided in the card.

I stopped feeling pity for my son and was able to only feel my love for him. I realized I needed to treat the situation with a firm, yet gentle assertion. I knew I needed to accept nothing but satisfaction in knowing my son was going to get the help he needed. By the time the counselor called me back I was able to talk to him with intelligence instead of anger, and we came up with a solution. My son has not been bullied since.

Situations like this, and even smaller ones, are the daily opportunities I have for using my angel cards, which are like a direct phone line to the angels. Sometimes the cards give me immediate answers, and sometimes suggestions that I need to focus and meditate on before the answer becomes clear. If you are like me and find mediation difficult because you never know what to focus on or can't quiet your mind, the cards give you something to focus on. Even if you don't have a specific situation or question in mind, simply pick a card and use it to be your focus during meditation and you will be surprised by the clarity and guidance you receive.

They are Waiting

Communication is not a one way street. You should ask, and even voice your opinion when you are connecting with your guides. You can do something as simple as pray or you can have your own special call when you want to get their attention. Imagine someone just sitting around waiting for you to call them; that is how angels can be to you. You will make them happy to have a little faith and put feeling strange aside to acknowledge their existence.

Sometimes your higher self will call for them without you knowing it. Very recently I had this happen to me. Some might say it was a dream, but I know it was not. I had been suffering with a horrible migraine. This was a monster of a migraine and it had lasted for days. I was not able to even get much sleep. I was hurting so badly I could not even think straight as to what I should do. I tried everything including taking medication. Nothing I tried worked. Finally, after about the end of the third day of suffering, I put the kids to bed and went to bed myself. Laying in bed, I felt as though my head were about to explode. I didn't even want to cry because I knew it would make the pain worse, but I couldn't help it. I lay in the dark feeling my tears flow from my eyes and wished I had the strength to pray or call out for help, but the pain was too intense. I knew it was going to be another sleepless night of horrifying pain.

As I closed my eyes I felt a comforting feeling start to come over me. It was a familiar feeling I remembered I had felt before. As a child when I had problems sleeping my mother would rub my forehead. This is what I felt then. I could actually feel the warmth of her hand touching my forehead. Instantly my headache was gone. I did not want to move out of fear my headache would return or that I would somehow be taken out of the moment. I could feel my hair move as it tickled my face. The thought came into my mind, "We are here to help you heal". The room was very quiet. It was so quite it started to feel as if the room and my mind were all one space. In my mind's eye I could see my mother standing next to me. It was out of the corner of my eye and I spotted her, though I stayed frozen not wanting this moment to end.

Once I saw her the room began to fill up with many more angels. I could feel them all around me; it felt like there were hundreds. I began to feel warmth cover my body. I have not felt such an overwhelming sense of peace ever before. At some point that evening everyone left and I was alone again. If it had not happened to me and I heard this story from someone else, part of me might think the pain caused the delusion, but it did happen to me and I do believe confidently in this. Undeniably, my pain was gone. I would say this is one of those times when desperation played a big part in what happened. I was so desperate for relief that ALL my beliefs fell away and anything was possible.

Observe your Dreams

You can analyze what happened to me all day long. Even if it was possible that I fell asleep, then I would just argue they communicated to me in my dreams. Angels do like to communicate in dreams to help give you clues and so you can see them. It is the perfect time to communicate because you are unlimited in your dreams. I give myself clues to help me know when I am dreaming so I am aware that I have no boundaries. My main clue is doors. When I dream now I look around at how the doors fit in the room. The doors will be smaller or a different shape than the actual door frame, which brings my attention to the fact that I am dreaming and can expected an unlimited experience in that dream. When you teach yourself to become aware of when you are dreaming, you can then have an additional experience. That is, when you're dreaming you can call in the people who you would like to see in your dream, including angels. Like I said in a previous chapter my mother rarely comes to me in dreams because of the disappointment I feel when I waken. Do not be disappointed if those you want to come to you in a dream don't; it is their way of protecting you from heartache.

Sometimes angels will communicate to you things they want you to do while in reality. As long as the message is one that is productive and helpful to you or someone else, then you should follow through with confidence. You will reap the rewards of furthering your communication with the angels and strengthening it. Angels are always watching and they will notice when you follow their guidance.

In conclusion, remember that contact and communication with your guides is as simple as just thinking about it and asking for it. Start by opening yourself and your beliefs so there is room for angels to come through. They are always waiting and hoping you will notice and they always notice you. Do not get disappointed or think they are not there because you think you can't see or hear them. Start by just asking for help from them to clear what is blocking you from getting their messages. If you keep trying and have patience in yourself, their love will come shining through. And as always, however it works for you and what you believe is the right way, the only way.

I will give you a couple of questions to think about. Is it possible you are like me and have had angels around you throughout your whole life? Have they been there so much that it just feels normal to you? If so, then you already have been communicating and they have been helping you. If not, remember that everything you need is already inside you. Ask for guidance to lift the veil which is hiding you from your experience in communicating with your guides and angels.

I asked my guides to help me change the perspective of someone who might not understand everything happens for a reason, even watching a loving mother pass away at such a young age. They gave me this perspective. I watched as my mother transformed her beliefs during her journey through cancer, but she never lost faith in God. Experiencing this with my mom opened my mind up to accept change in beliefs. I realized then as I know now beliefs can be changed, but faith is strong. This kind of knowing will get me through the rest of my life.

Epilogue

Nearly 28 years have passed since I last saw my mother, physically. Our connection before she physically left me was strong and I know she didn't want to leave me; yet, in a beautiful turn of events, amazingly, the connection I have with her now is even stronger. We didn't arrive at this overnight, though. For a very long time I felt no connection with her at all, mostly due to the way I handled the pain that comes with abandonment through death and the limited beliefs I collected during my life. In many ways, the feelings of abandonment left me feeling sorry for myself and I was at the bottom of a pit of depression and sorrow for a very long time.

Through the process of transitioning from the depths of my despair to knowing that my connection with my mother is now stronger than ever, I have learned that things will usually get much worse before we will turn that corner and see things begin to get better. I also learned I would not have made it past the low points without the protection and guidance of my angels who continually worked behind the scenes to make sure sue I was always learning and growing, no matter how bad things felt.

People hold a variety of beliefs about angels. Some believe they are entities who are here to help us; some believe angels are part of our superconscious mind only. Regardless, the important thing is that you know they are there. I don't have all the answers about how to transform limited beliefs created by death and arrive at a place where I know without a doubt that I am supported by the angels, but I do know how the process begins. That is, I began to thrive when I discovered how to communicate with my guides, including my mom.

The words of the poem I've included below describe the essence of my experience beautifully and are written by a man who knew all too well about death and what it means to live with the limited beliefs caused by watching loved ones die.

I wish you all the best in your own journey of discovery and I know the angels will guide you along the way.

Alone

Edgar Allan Poe

From childhood's hour I have not been
As others were; I have not seen
As others saw; I could not bring
My passions from a common spring.

From the same source I have not taken
My sorrow; I could not awaken
My heart to joy at the same tone;
And all I loved, I loved alone.

Then - in my childhood, in the dawn
Of a most stormy life - was drawn
From every depth of good and ill
The mystery which binds me still:

From the torrent, or the fountain,
From the red cliff of the mountain,
From the sun that round me rolled
In its autumn tint of gold,
From the lightning in the sky
As it passed me flying by,
From the thunder and the storm,
And the cloud that took the form
(When the rest of Heaven was blue)
Of a demon in my view